Here's what experts are saying about 20/20 Brain Power

"Of all the books on brain health and fitness, 20/20 Brainpower illuminates one of the most overlooked fundamentals: mental speed and flexibility. Joshua Reynolds takes us on a journey into practical yet scientifically backed dietary, nutritional, and lifestyle solutions with compelling reasons why we cannot afford to leave our potential for brilliance to mere chance. It's a delight to read."

Michael A. Schmidt, Ph.D.
Research Associate, NASA Ames Research Center, author of Brain-Building Nutrition and the textbook, *Nutritional Pharmacology and Clinical Neuroscience.*

"20/20 Brain Power is the equivalent of an Olympic training program for the mind. Faster brains correlate with increased intelligence and healthier, longer lives. The information and brain exercises in 20/20 Brain Power are so important that I have begun to incorporate them into my seminars on anti-aging and life extension. Everyone can benefit from this program."

Ross Pelton, R.Ph., Ph.D., CCN
Author, *Mind Food & Smart Pills*, and *The Drug-Induced Nutrient Depletion Handbook.*

"An outstanding contribution to the field of cognitive assessment and enhancement! Fascinating new information--valuable for anyone interested in keeping and improving their mental edge and longevity!

Jacqueline Marcell, author of *Elder Rage*

"The bad news is, our brains lose function with age. The good news it that 20/20 Brain Power can help you regain and maintain your brain! In a clear, user friendly way Joshua Reynolds does an amazing job of explaining how the brain works and how we can optimize its health and performance as we age - including practical brain exercises, foods and supplements to keep our mind sharp and memory strong!"

Hyla Cass, MD
Assistant Clinical Professor of Psychiatry
U.C.L.A. School of Medicine, Los Angeles, CA
Author, *8 Weeks To Vibrant Health, and Natural Highs*

"The promising potential of the recent scientific revival of brain speed is invitingly augured in this very clearly and entertainingly written book by Joshua Reynolds, a pioneer in the modern technology of brain speed science. His exposition of the importance of mental speed in everyday life provides an engaging introduction for lay persons and indicates further avenues for exploration by present-day researchers."

Arthur R. Jensen, Ph.D.
Professor Emeritus
University of California, Berkeley

"20/20 Brain Power brilliantly reveals how our speeded up world is slowing us down - mentally and physically. The beauty is that 20/20 offers a quick and practical way to upgrade our powers of concentration, memory and mental agility."

Marcus Laux, N.D.
Adj. Faculty, Bastyr Univ., Editor, Naturally Well Today
Co-author *Natural Woman, Natural Menopause*

"The 20/20 program of mental exercise, diet, nutritional supplementation and self assessment tools can empower almost anyone to take charge of their brain health and fitness. I can and have recommended it with confidence to all those who want to be pro-active in their health and fitness."

Bruce Kovacs, M.D.
Keck School of Medicine, U.S.C.

"Many of us lead lives that are less than 'brain-friendly'. Fortunately, help is on the way in the form of the 20/20 Brain Power program, developed by Joshua Reynolds. Much as people have come to accept regular trips to the gym as important for maintaining physical fitness and health, we can expect that mental tune-ups will become an increasingly important part of modern life. Joshua Reynolds is to be congratulated on putting together this ground-breaking and challenging program."

Gerald Matthews, Ph.D.
Professor, Dept. of Psychology
University of Cincinnati

"Very few, if any, regardless of their degrees or experience, understand the brain and cognitive function better than Joshua Reynolds. 20/20 Brain Power is essential reading for anyone who wants to understand more about their brain's performance and learn how to enhance it."

L Cass Terry, M.D., Ph.D., Pharm.D., MBA
Former Chair and Professor of Neurology, Medical College of Wisconsin, WI

"Joshua Reynolds has pioneered the development of the next generation of cognitive measurement - brain speed - a quantum leap beyond most conventional neuro-psych tests. He has also uniquely turned these tests into brain exercises. It's true for the body, but "use it or lose it" may be even more important for saving your brain."

Vernon Mark, M.D., FACS
Associate Professor of Surgery, Harvard Medical School (Ret.); Director Emeritus Neurosurgery, Boston City Hospital, author *Brainpower and Reversing Memory Loss*

"20/20 Brain Power is a wonderfully comprehensive program founded on the most advanced and respected research in brain science. Joshua Reynolds provides a unique and user-friendly approach not only to maintaining brain health, but enhancing function as well."

David Perlmutter, M.D., FACN
Author, *The Better Brain Book*

"Joshua Reynolds' book, 20/20 Brain Power is a unique and comprehensive program founded on the latest brain and cognitive research. The book provides a unique approach for mental exercise, diet, nutritional supplementation and self-assessment tools. As a geriatrician I feel everyone, irrespective of their age, is now empowered to take charge of their brain health and fitness."

Yogesh Shah, M.D., FAAFP, CMD
Mercy/Mayo Clinic

20/20 Brain Power

by
Joshua Reynolds

With
Robert Heller, MD

20/20 Brain Power

Written by: Joshua Reynolds
                    Robert Heller, MD

ISBN: 0-9767633-0-3

First Printing, April 2005
Second Printing, September 2007

Published by
20/20 Brain Power Partners, LLC
Laguna Beach, CA

www.2020brainpower.com

Printed in the Unites States of America

The contents of this book are general guidelines for diet, exercise and supplementation for good brain health. It is not a substitute for regular visits to your health care provider. Periodic check-ups are essential for maintaining good health. Everyone is different and everyone may respond differently to the diet, exercise and supplementation recommendations describe in this book. Speak to your health care provider about the recommendations in this book and work together to make the choices that are best for you.

This book is dedicated to anyone: who may fear for their ultimate brain health, fitness and longevity; who may want to age-proof their brain and increase their cognitive reserves to protect their brain against the ravages of aging; who may desire to gain, or re-gain and maintain their powers of memory, concentration and thinking; who may want to generate and sustain optimal brain power in their professional as well as personal life pursuits, and; who may be ready for a fun and easy lifestyle approach to help reduce the risk of cognitive impairment and ensure the possibility of a lifetime of optimal brain health and fitness.

Table of Contents

Acknowledgments

Discovery is rarely an isolated, individual event. In most cases, such as mine, other individuals form nodes in the nexus of a cocreative group mind. I have been extremely fortunate in attracting some of the brightest men and women for my research and work in the brain sciences. Their brilliant minds have fanned the flames of my curiosity and helped me better understand the complexities of the brain, the mind, and the body. Without their encouragement and support 20/20 Brain Power might never have come to be.

First I would like to acknowledge and thank one of the premier cognitive scientists and psychologists of our time – Arthur Jensen, PhD, Professor Emeritus, University of California. Berkeley. The world's acknowledged expert on brainpower, speed, and intelligence, Dr. Jensen has been selfless, open, and abundantly generous with his time and knowledge. My heartfelt thanks to you, Art.

I am also deeply grateful to Richard Haier, PhD, a superb cognitive scientist and psychologist at the University of California, Irvine Medical School. Dr. Haier is one of the leading and most highly published authorities on the use of PET scan and MRI images of the brain to better understand intelligence and cognitive function. Thank you, Rich, for sharing your remarkable breakthroughs and insights.

To my good friend Cass Terry, MD, PhD, PharmD, a resounding thank-you for so willingly and graciously sharing your knowledge with me. Dr. Terry was the Chairman of the Department of Neurology at the Medical College of Wisconsin. As a brilliant researcher, clinician, and teacher, he is one of the pioneers in body and brain antiaging science.

Vernon Mark, MD, former Director of Neurosurgery at Boston City Hospital and Professor of Surgery at Harvard Medical School, has been a rich and plentiful source of information. His books, Brainpower and Reversing Memory Loss, are must-reads for anyone interested in brain maintenance and brainpower building. What I admire most about Dr. Mark is that he walks his talk. Approaching 80 he still has a remarkably quick and sharp mind that is also quite long on humor. Thank you, Vern.

I am especially grateful to the late Jonas Salk, MD, founder of the Salk Institute. Jonas was an ardent student of the outer realms of reality, and human nature and its ultimate potential. What he taught me and many others who frequently gathered at his beautiful home in La Jolla, California, far transcended conventional wisdom in medicine. He was a great friend and a plentiful source of information. His inspiration lingers still.

There are so many others I would like to thank: Ruth O'Hara, Ph.D. of Stanford University, for example, understands Alzheimer's and Mild Cognitive Impairment as well as anyone; Hyla Cass, MD, of the University of California, Los Angeles, who has not only been a great inspiration over the years but whose profound and prolific mind has churned out over six books including her latest, 8 Weeks To Vibrant Health; and, of course, my personal brain-mind guru, Yogesh Shah, MD, of the Mercy/Mayo Clinic. Thank you, Yogi, for introducing me to a refreshing, open-minded, and comprehensive insight into the causes and possible cures for premature and accelerated memory decline. Indeed, I would like to thank all of the scientists, clinicians, and researchers I have worked with over the years.

Thanks also to my dear friend, personal physician par excellence, wonderful partner, and medical director, Robert Heller, MD. Without your constant support, if not coercion, I might still be stuck in the doldrums of mediocrity.

Thank you, thank you, to Christine Macgenn Rodgerson, the writer who turned my erudite cognitive colloquialisms into an enjoyable, informative, inspirational read. Many of our beta testers who read your final draft have called it a real page-turner. Christine, you are brilliant.

To my accomplished, ingenious, and talented business partner, John Arnold, it is a long-awaited pleasure to finally work with someone as positive and powerful as you are. Thank you for helping me to materialize my dream.

Last, but first in my heart, I am eternally grateful to my loving, patient, and amazingly supportive family. To my children, Christina, Myriah, and Jonah, you have been my steadfast support and inspiration. Thank you for letting me spend so many long hours writing and researching when I could have been reading you bedtime stories, driving you to soccer practice, and helping you with your homework. And, to my loving great friends and siblings, Brad, and sister, Martha, and to you dear mother, Mary – you have waited 87 years for this. Thanks for your continual support.

To my wife Barbara, my true soul mate, thank you for being such a steady, gracious, and loving partner, and mom, while I disappeared behind my 17-inch monitor for the past dozen years. And here we are!

Foreword

Several years ago I met Joshua Reynolds at a medical convention where he was demonstrating his unique brain speed tests. There was a long line of physicians and scientists waiting to participate. My curiosity and interest in neuroscience, particularly memory and cognition, motivated me to wait my turn and see for myself what his tests were all about.

After my test I realized that I had just experienced a major breakthrough in brain science. Joshua Reynolds had developed an objective method for measuring mental performance, as well as brain health, using computerized tests of brain processing speed. As science had proven, a person's brain speed reflects how quickly memories can be recalled, questions answered, problems solved, and decisions made. In effect, brain speed determines how efficiently the mind works. It is scientifically correlated with IQ, memory, focus, success, and even longevity.

Primary care physicians had never had such a simple yet accurate measure of cognitive function and memory, especially in the early stages of decline. Alzheimer's is a process that can begin 30 or 40 years before it is diagnosed. Yet we in the medical community have had no practical way to identify it until very late in its progression. In that moment I realized that these tests were a way of detecting those early stages of mental decline while there was still time to intervene.

As a result of testing many thousands of brains, Joshua Reynolds had developed an understanding of the global brain that was seemingly escaping the rest of the scientific community. It appeared that the average brain was slowing down, way down. In fact, according to the data it seemed that we were in the midst of an apparent epidemic of what Josh termed premature mental decline, or PMD.

Joshua's background in biofeedback enabled him to also develop a brain speed exercise program designed to increase brainpower and improve memory and attention span, or focus, in response to the rising need for early detection and prevention. The applications for this new technology struck me as obvious. Students, young professionals, baby boomers, and even seniors all looking for a way to maintain their mental edge and memory now would have a practical way to do it. Just as the physical fitness revolution was born out of new exercise technology in the seventies, I had a sense that I was witnessing a historic advance in brain health and fitness technology.

I knew when I met Josh that I had found a kindred spirit. I had spent many years in my medical practice actively pursuing the most advanced and effective treatments for my patients. Here was someone doing the same in the field of brain and mind health. It was a pleasure to form a partnership with him.

An ardent researcher, and brilliant technologist and inventor, Joshua Reynolds has been on a mission to change the way we think about, and especially care for, the brain, a mission I have been fortunate and proud to become a part of. Not only has he pioneered the field of brain speed testing and training, but he has also been able to use his technologies to determine what truly works and what doesn't when it comes to dietary and supplemental nutrition for the brain.

It all comes down to a simple premise when you think about it. Give your brain what it needs and it will perform wonderfully for a lifetime. Deprive it of what it needs and it will slow down, begin to malfunction, and eventually be greatly diminished. Joshua Reynolds' 20/20 Brain Power Program incorporates his brain speed and memory building exercises, super brain nutrition, proven brain performance supplements, and stress reduction techniques to enhance brainpower, and boost mental clarity and energy. Brain health and fitness can improve mood and induce deep, restful sleep.

In the past, I had no answers for my patients who asked for help with their memory problems. Now I can recommend the 20/20 Brain Power Program. This program is the most comprehensive approach to brain health and fitness that I know of. However, I found that it is actually even more than that. It is a call to action and I urge you to heed that call. I did and it has changed my life, and the lives of my patients.

Robert Heller, MD

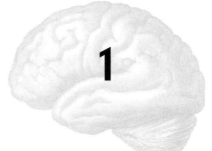

The Journey to 20/20 Brain Power

"The incredible thing about the human mind is that it did not come with an instruction book."

Terry Riley

Some years ago I had started to worry about my memory. Who hasn't? Those subtle little moments when you feel tongue-tied, have lost a word or a name, or forgotten where you put something. We often dismiss these subtle signs of aging as little irritations, and we try to ignore them. However, for me these little senior moments started me on a journey…the journey to 20/20 Brain Power.

Sometimes the exquisite timing of certain events can dramatically alter the course of a person's life. In 1994 two seemingly unrelated experiences did just that to mine.

I have been an inventor most of my life. I am naturally curious – about life and human nature and potential. Some of my inventions, like the Mood Ring and the ThighMaster, were actually developed, tested, and marketed as self-help tools. I never expected the ring to take off as a fad, especially since I designed the original stress card it was based on as a real biofeedback barometer of mood and stress levels. Today stress cards are used by millions of people in corporate and medically sponsored stress management programs. The ThighMaster also became a fad, but its rapid muscle toning action was based on innovative exercise science called dynamic resistance. I didn't know it then, but this understanding of the way a muscle responds to exercise would later help me intuit how to develop brain speed exercise techniques and technology.

Discovery excites me. It usually starts with a burning question, just like the one that blazed through my mind on my 53rd birthday when my beautiful wife, Barbara, announced that I was going to be a father, again. Of course, I had the normal questions coursing through my head. Will it be a boy or a girl? Will he or she be healthy and whole? How will I adjust to the coming years of sleep deprivation? My bladder was already causing me enough lost REM sleep. Visions of Little League and soccer practice started dancing in my head. "Better hit the weights and aerobic classes," my younger friends teased.

Then I remembered hearing that our local school system was doing calculus in grade school and I began to panic. At my very core I worried, "How will I keep up mentally with my child?" Even though my SAT math score was pretty good, the calculating part of my brain was now beginning to feel a bit rusty and slow.

As the universe would have it, right after my wife's blessed announcement, I happened to read a Life magazine cover story called "Building A Better Brain." Think faster, improve your memory, and defend against Alzheimer's disease were the claims boldly inked across the cover. The article told of 80- and 90-year-old nuns who engaged in daily brain games to stay mentally sharp and physically fit. But, there was more to the story than that. Somehow their brain exercises were also adding more healthy years to their lives.

While I was reading the article, I flashed back to something that happened when I was in high school and just getting started with my first entrepreneurial adventure, The Atlas Barbell Company. "Working out with weights will make you muscle-bound and slow you down," my football coach told me, which was what everyone thought about weight lifting back in the sixties. Boy, were they wrong. Today, with the aid of power-building exercise techniques and technology, even gangly, 135-pound teenagers can turn themselves into hulking NFL linebackers.

It was right then, in the midst of my preparental walk down memory lane that I wondered, "If weight lifting builds muscle power, then what builds brainpower?" And therein lies the burning question that began my journey to 20/20 Brain Power.

Mental Muscles

When you use weights or other resistance training techniques to build muscle size and power, you are essentially stimulating the muscle's motor neurons to fire more rapidly. This stimulation of the motor neuron causes the muscle to grow. I began to ponder whether or not the same analogy would hold true in the brain. Maybe challenging brain cells to work harder and faster could make the brain stronger, sharper, and smarter. I decided to make some inquiries. I sought out the brightest minds in the fields of cognitive psychology, neuroscience, and intelligence and I was awed by what I learned.

I discovered that the key to mental ability, or intelligence, lies in something called elementary cognitive processes (ECPs), which are measurable subcomponents of thinking. A thought, you see, is made up of several ECPs. Each performs a discrete task, such as registering or reading incoming information, storing and later retrieving it, reasoning, making decisions, and sometimes taking actions based on those choices. I began wondering if exercising these ECPs and stimulating more brain cells into action would result in smarter thinking, better memory, and greater mental productivity.

To test any theory, especially in behavior, you have to be able to measure the effects you are looking for; in this case, changes in brainpower. "You can't manage what you can't measure," some of my cognitive scientist associates used to say.

Working with an extraordinary team of computer science, brain, and intelligence experts I designed and patented a series of computerized tasks that challenged and measured the performance of different ECPs. Determining the processing speed of each of them could give us an objective, overall measurement of brainpower. Perhaps brainpower was simply speed. I sensed I was on to something.

Now all we needed were enough subjects (mental guinea pigs) to test. We needed a Website with international pull. Through the Internet we could test thousands of brains. We could build a database of test results demonstrating how the average brain performs, especially in terms of speed, memory, and intelligence. By offering a battery of my brain speed tests disguised as fun, yet challenging, brain games we could collect a wealth of cognitive data. That was when we developed the largest brain-related site on the World Wide Web.

Thousands upon thousands of curious minds from all over the world took my IQ, brain speed, and memory tests. Once we had gathered and crunched the data, we were able to compare young brains with middle-aged and old brains, brains in one profession with brains in another, rich brains, poor brains, working class brains and artistic brains, one country's collective brain with that of another. We were perhaps the first group in history to view the global brain. It was a thrilling moment.

However, as we studied the layers upon layers of data, what we learned was shocking. The data was exposing a seemingly natural, yet steep rate of decline in brainpower as we age. Under a demanding mental challenge, including the pressure to perform a task quickly, the brain's speed of performance slows down at an amazing rate. In fact, by age 55 we lose on average approximately 50 percent of our brainpower (speed). This was even more startling when we realized that our data had shown that the average web user's IQ score was 15 to 20 points higher than the general population.

What was happening? What was causing this rapid loss of brain speed and memory power in so many people? Why was it occurring so much more rapidly than the decline in our physical reflexes and muscle strength? Had we uncovered a previously unnoticed yet obviously common brain health epidemic? These questions only fueled my obsession to learn more.

Exercising Your Mind

Shortly thereafter I read a university research study that showed that only a few days of brain speed exercise enabled old rats to perform specific tasks at a rate equal to that of much younger rats. A microscopic look inside the dissected rat craniums showed a significant growth of new brain cells, and connections called axons and dendrites. Now everything was starting to add up. Maybe those nuns from the Life cover story had learned through experience what neuroscience was just discovering – that the old adage "use it or lose it" applies to the brain, too. Perhaps even more than it does to the body.

My brain speed tests were designed to measure and analyze brainpower, including physical reflexes, brain speed, memory, attention, and executive thinking processes. From my background in biofeedback I wondered if these tests could also be used to stimulate brain cells via a cognitive workout. I wondered if brain speed training might actually build brainpower. By again using the World Wide Web we presented the tests as brain speed games to thousands of participants. They were asked to play the games repetitively and quickly. We found that my hunch was right. The use of these brain stimulation games yielded a dramatic improvement in brainpower, defined as the brain's information processing speed, or brain speed, in as little as 20 days.

In a subsequent clinical trial in Texas my computerized, interactive brain speed exercises were administered to a group of 50 people ranging in age from 15 to 70 and older. Half the group trained daily for 21 days with my brain speed exercises while the control group did nothing. Everyone was tested for IQ, anxiety level, and attention at the beginning and end of the 21-day period. Remarkably, the group that did my daily brain speed games improved almost 10 points in IQ compared to the nontraining, control group. They also showed significant improvements in focused attention and concentration, and were less anxious in their lives compared to the control group.

As remarkable as this quick increase in brainpower was, I could not help but wonder what would happen if we went back to the weight lifting paradigm for yet another piece of the puzzle. Weight training combined with the nutritional support of muscle-building supplements, such as the powerful branched-chain amino acids, can significantly increase muscle power. Everyone from gymnasts to sprinters, from ice skaters to ski jumpers was improving their competitive edge (and even breaking world records) by synergistically combining rigorous resistance training with potent muscle-building nutrients, such as whey protein powder. Maybe the same would hold true for the brain.

Nourishing Your Brain

I read every brain nutrition study I could find and consulted with every published brain neurochemistry professor I could get to return my call or e-mail. This is when I met Dr. Robert Heller, a UCLA professor and internist who combined nutritional and medical science to provide his patients with a more holistic and preventative form of health care. He had focused much of his attention on the brain and greatly aided me in my understanding of brain health and fitness. What was even more interesting was that when I tested Dr. Heller's brain for quickness he scored above the fastest group of people, who were also more than 30 years younger. That convinced me that he walked his talk, and could help me better understand the relationship among brain speed and health, memory, and maybe even longevity (which has recently been confirmed).

I began to see the brain from a whole new perspective. I realized that in the same way the body can't function without the nutrients it needs, neither can the brain. Brain fatigue, forgetfulness, confusion, anxiety, and disease can all be symptoms of basic brain starvation. It was so clear — the brain needs nourishment. Just like the body, it needs proteins, carbohydrates, fats, and more than a dash of fruits and vegetables. More specifically, it needs brain-essential amino acids, fatty acids and phospholipids, and antioxidant-rich fruits and vegetables to fuel, support, protect, and preserve its precious neurons.

I tracked down research scientists in brain biochemistry and met with cognitive scientists who were studying the brain's intelligence, or processing efficiency, with Positron Emission Tomography, or PET scans – imaging machines that monitor brain cell activity, or metabolism. I met other scientists and researchers who were increasing brain processing speed through the use of vital neural nutrients, some derived from plants and herbs like ginkgo, daffodil, and periwinkle; others from pharmaceutical agents called nootropics, such as Piracetam, approved as smart drugs in much of Europe.

As I began putting all of this new information together and testing it out, I found that brain speed training worked even better when a person's brain cells were properly nourished. When the brain is given the nutrients it needs it responds almost immediately with improved power, speed, and performance.

But there was still one piece of the puzzle missing. Like any muscle in the body the brain can do only so much hard work before it gets tired and starts losing efficiency. When your brain is fatigued you are not going to be at your best. A fatigued brain is forgetful, foggy, and spaced-out. When your brain is overwrought you feel drained, irritable, and inefficient. You no longer have the brain energy you need to stay sharp, alert, active, and aware. So what is a tired brain to do? I found the answer when I went back to my roots in biofeedback and stress management. In fact, I had one of those aha moments.

The Stress Factor

Over the years I had developed, tested, and perfected something I call an Alpha Brain Break, a quick way of deeply quieting the mind and stilling the brain. In the same way that a time-out or a nap can be a lifesaver for a child whose brain is reeling from too much stimulation, an Alpha Brain Break can de-stress your brain and restore your mind's full capacity and natural brilliance. I witnessed the effects of Alpha Brain Breaks in all of the people who came to my stress management clinic to learn brainwave control. Electroencephalograph (EEG) machines show that during a 10- to 15-minute alpha-break the brain quickly unwinds – possibly releasing more accumulated stress than during a whole night's sleep. This clears the mind, recharges the brain cells, and prepares the brain for optimal performance.

I soon found that combining an Alpha Brain Break with brain speed exercising and specific brain-nourishing nutrition rapidly improved brainpower, mental clarity, and quickness. There is a tremendous synergy between these three forms of brain care.

20/20 Brain Power

In the same way that 20/20 vision means that you have superior visual processing and acuity, 20/20 brainpower means that you have superior mental processing and acuity. And, just as a corrective eye lens or Lasik surgery can adjust poor or compromised vision, corrective cognitive enhancement tools and techniques can convert poor memory, fuzzy-headedness, and slow thinking into 20/20 brainpower.

As a result of my research I have come to understand that the brain has three essential needs that must be satisfied every day. Fulfilling these needs yields sustainable brain health and fitness, with optimal mental performance when you demand it. Ignoring these needs can cause a premature decline in brainpower, and overall mental health and fitness. My goal in writing 20/20 Brain Power and developing the 20-day 20/20 Brain Power Program is to give you everything you need to nourish, support, and protect your brain – for life.

My experience in brain speed assessment and enhancement has led me to a somewhat iconoclastic belief that anyone can regenerate his or her brainpower (speed), and improve mental performance, concentration, and memory, no matter how old he or she is. Embrace the powerful cognitive health, fitness, and performance-enhancing tools in this book with your heart as well as your mind and you will reduce your brain stress and increase your mental quickness, acuity, and memory. Try my Program; it takes only 20 minutes a day for 20 days. You will experience noticeable improvements in your ability to focus your attention. You will learn and recall information more quickly, and make decisions and solve problems faster and more accurately.

The mandate is clear. A sharp, calm, high-performance mind needs a fit and healthy brain to sustain itself throughout the day, and for the rest of your life. Let's get started. Let's get you on the road to 20/20 Brain Power, right now.

2

The Need for Speed

We live in a moment of history where change is so speeded up that we begin to see the present only when it is already disappearing."

R. D. Laing

There is nothing quite as disconcerting as being in a difficult situation, unable to focus or control your thoughts. There is nothing worse than losing your mental edge in front of others. Forgetting your PIN number and holding up a long line in front of an ATM machine, forgetting your boss's wife's name when you are introducing her to someone, or where you parked your car can all be quite embarrassing, if not alarming. Whether you are on the tennis court, making a sales call, applying for a new job, or seated in a boardroom, feeling sharp, looking smart, and performing well are what we all want and what we all strive for. Knowledge, wisdom, and experience are the very essence of our lives. But, what good are they if names, words, and ideas get stuck on the tip of your tongue, or lost in a mental fog?

Slight lapses in memory have long been pooh-poohed as nothing serious, just something we all go through eventually. Who hasn't experienced those embarrassing little moments of forgetfulness, misplaced keys, lost words, missed birthdays, or forgotten names? When those seemingly insignificant memory failures happen in our 20s it barely breaks our stride. When it happens after 40 it frequently launches us into fear that we might end up losing our minds. Well, our fears may be warranted. Here is what we know: Our brains may be in trouble, deep trouble.

Over 4 million people in America have Alzheimer's disease. This number is projected to exceed 15 million in the not-too-distant future. In the aging population the statistics become even more troubling – five to 10 percent of the population older than 60 and half of those older than 85 will get Alzheimer's. That means if you reach the age of 85 for the rest of your life you have a 50/50 chance of developing this dreaded disease. But that is only the beginning of the Alzheimer's story.

We now know that Alzheimer's does not just happen. It is actually the end of a long journey, one that can begin as early as when we are in our late 20s or early 30s. That's right. The degenerative process that leads to Alzheimer's disease can begin in the brain as many as 30 to 40 years before it is clinically diagnosed.

Mild cognitive impairment, or MCI, is a recently recognized brain condition now believed to be a precursor to Alzheimer's. It is suspected that 20 million or more Americans may already be suffering from MCI. The only symptom of MCI is seemingly benign forgetfulness. Unless it is detected and treated early on, studies have found that MCI progresses to Alzheimer's in eight out of 10 people within five to 10 years. But MCI doesn't just happen either. It appears to be preceded by suboptimal mental performance and something I call premature mental decline, or PMD.

PMD is the result of a decrease in the brain's ability to efficiently and swiftly process information – brain speed. Brain speed is your brain's velocity — how fast it processes what is going on around and within you. Your brain speed determines how rapidly you can scrutinize information, recall recently learned information, make the right split-second decision, and then take the necessary action quickly and appropriately.

Fuzzy thinking, mental fog, brain strain, and senior moments can all be symptoms of PMD, and caused by compromised brain speed. Global statistics show that as many as one-third of the people older than 40 — that is one out of every three — are experiencing a steep and significant decline in mental performance and brain speed as they age.

High-Velocity Brain

The executive headquarters of the brain, located right behind the forehead and between the temples, works like a computer processor. The faster it processes information the more you can learn and the faster you can remember. Studies have shown that the faster your brain's processing speed the higher your IQ, the quicker your responses and reactions, the more successful you are in your world. The speedier your brain, the more aware you are. And, the faster your brain processes what is going on in your life, the clearer and calmer your mind.

Imagine you are speeding down a busy freeway, your children are in the back seat, your cell phone is ringing, and the car in front of you suddenly starts spinning out of control. What do you do? Hit the breaks? Accelerate? Swerve left? Swerve right? How quickly and effectively can you make this life-and-death decision? That depends on how fast your brain is processing what is happening.

In less time than it takes to form a thought your brain has to perceive what is happening, remember similar events, as well as what you have learned about those events, process all of your potential responses, formulate a decision, and then command the right muscles to immediately take the appropriate action — fast. Everything that happens inside you, and to you, is processed by and through your brain. How efficiently and effectively it all works depends (mainly) on the speed with which the various parts of your brain communicate with each other and with your body.

A world-class athlete displays the ultimate in both mental and physical quickness. His or her high-velocity brain speed makes it possible to hold many options in mind and play them out, or process them quite rapidly. The faster the processing the more likely the choices and plays are to be winners. A quarterback on Super Bowl Sunday, for example, has to scan the field, dodge the oncoming rush of mean-spirited lineman and ferocious linebackers, play out all the practical options, and then decide whether or not to throw the ball, where to throw it, or if he should duck and run. If he is in "the zone" then all that exists is direct experience and action. The information is flowing through his brain's processing centers without effort. No time is wasted on stopping to think about it. All of his cognitive calculations are taking place in milliseconds, far faster than it takes to form a single thought. If he has to stop and think about what he is doing, the other quarterback gets the ring.

Everything you do depends on your brain speed. Your job, your paycheck, your relationships, even your health can depend on how sharp and fit you keep your brain. Brain speed determines attention, alertness, learning, memory, decision making, problem solving, and even mental clarity. The faster your brain is processing the quicker you can think and respond – successfully. The speedier your brain, the more aware you are, the more information you can take in. You are processing more sensory input, faster. When your mind doesn't have to search and struggle for information it can solve problems more easily, more quickly, and more efficiently, with less stress.

Over 50 years of cognitive research and testing have shown that the brain's processing speed is highly indicative of its health and fitness. In fact, brain speed measurement may be more accurate, objective, and reliable indicator of brainpower than any other noninvasive type of measurement. What's more, processing speed is a highly sensitive marker of the brain's reaction to pharmaceutical drugs, as well as natural therapies including exercise, neural nutrition, stimulation, and relaxation. The trend in scientific research now is focusing more and more on brain speed and how to preserve and enhance it.

Brain Speed As You Age

Brain performance data shows that the brain's information processing speed declines significantly faster than the body's physical reaction time, or reflexes. This suggests that our brains may indeed be aging faster than our bodies. Put another more dramatic way, when you are 60 you might have tight abs and firm thighs, yet not be able to remember the names of those you love. A classic example, former U.S. President Ronald Reagan, fell and broke his hip at the age of 89. Still physically strong in spite of his Alzheimer's disease, Reagan's hip mended like a much younger man's. But, in spite of his physical strength at that time, his mind was still lost forever to his family and friends.

Figure 2.1 shows what happens to the speed of our mental and physical reactions as we age. The top line represents the age-related decline in physical reflexes, a medically accepted marker of biological age and rate of aging. The middle line represents the decline in a simple yes or no choice reaction time, such as the decision to run a yellow light or hit the brakes. The bottom line represents the decline in time it takes to make a complex decision, with a variety of possible actions, such as whether to hit the brakes or accelerate, or swerve right or left when you are unexpectedly faced with a stalled car in your lane on the freeway.

Age Related Decline in Brainpower (speed)

Figure 2.1*

I have defined brain speed in what I call milliHertz, as indicated in Figures 2.1, 2.2, and 2.3. It is inversely related to time, that is, the millisecond measure of mental and physical reaction times. One million milliHertz equals 1 millisecond. Ten thousand milliHertz equals 100 milliseconds. One thousand milliHertz equals 1,000 milliseconds, or one second of reaction speed time. By the way, don't worry – you don't have to remember these conversions!

As you can see, as we age, when we are confronted with challenging decisions, caught by surprise, forced to multitask, or solve a problem fast, especially when we are under pressure, quick responses become harder and harder. Our ability to perform them becomes slower and slower because we are losing brain speed. But is this decline in speed inevitable? It is not. Just like you can upgrade the processing speed of your computer, you can upgrade the processing speed of your brain.

Your Bio-Computer

A computer has a hard drive, a processor, and memory. The hard drive is where long-term information is stored. The computer's central processing unit is commonly known as its CPU. Random access memory, or RAM, is information that is dynamically held for short periods of time. The CPU requests the data it needs from RAM, processes it, and writes new data back to RAM in a continuous cycle. You have probably heard the expression "you can never be too rich." Well, in the world of computers, you can never have too much RAM. Next to your processor, RAM is most vital to performance.

Your brain also has RAM. Cognitive scientists call it working memory. It is literally the executive headquarters of your brain, and it is changing every minute. Stored memories are retrieved and new information is temporarily being held in mind while it is being used. And in the same way that the CPU, RAM, and hard drive in a computer are continually communicating, the various parts of your brain are in constant dialogue with each other, and with the rest of your body. The faster your brain's processing speed the clearer the communication and the better the results.

Let's say you are at work, and you are about to order take-out for lunch. Right at the moment you are searching for the telephone number to your favorite restaurant one of your colleagues asks you to please order something for her. Just then, another coworker calls out his order, and then someone else decides she wants something, too. Brain RAM makes it possible for you to store the phone number and all of your colleagues' menu selections while you dial the phone and place the order. The faster your brain speed the better your ability to remember it all, and the less likely you are to have to ask your friends to repeat their orders.

286 Or Pentium IV

Have you ever been using a computer when it just stops and freezes? Often what is happening is that the processor cannot handle the amount of information it is processing, so the computer starts thrashing. The screen starts blinking and the words and images on it begin fragmenting. Then the computer crashes. It stops and waits, hoping to clear the pathways so the information can get through, and the processor can begin working efficiently again. The faster your computer's processor the less likely this is to happen.

Imagine that you have to make a very important presentation at work. For weeks beforehand you are utterly stressed – you work long hours worried that you won't make the deadline. You eat poorly, mostly on the run. You get less and less sleep as the day approaches. Even when you are asleep your brain is not truly at rest. Your mind is busy thinking and fretting. Your stress hormone levels are off the charts day in and day out.

Finally the day of the presentation arrives. Everyone is seated at the conference table – the management team, your boss, and many of your coworkers. You set up your laptop; the presentation should come off without a hitch. But instead, there is that small glitch. You know the one. The computer freezes, the slide presentation comes to a screeching halt and no matter what you do, nothing works. The harder you try, the worse it gets. You try to reboot, but it doesn't work. You look helplessly around the room. You don't know what to do. One of your younger, seemingly sharper and quicker colleagues has to bail you out. You are frazzled, embarrassed, and you fumble little bits of the presentation for the next hour-and-a half, forgetting important dates, names, and locations. What is going on?

You are experiencing working memory breakdown. It is not your lack of knowledge or even intelligence that is sputtering; it is the stress overload in your brain that is slowing it down. Your brain does not have the processing speed it needs to handle all of the information coming in or the challenges it is facing. Of course, emotional pressure also has a lot to do with this slowdown.

Brain Speed Shows

How successfully you register and discriminate information, input, encode, organize, and retrieve it, and how fast you can manipulate that information to make a decision, and then react or act on it are ALL contingent on your brain's processing speed. How important is processing speed? Speed is everything.

Speed is smart. IQ test scores correlate highly with brain processing speed, in other words, quicker is smarter. Speed is logical. Working memory or executive decision-making speed has been scientifically equated with logic and reasoning power. Speed is healthy. The faster your brain, the healthier you are. In fact, faster brains live longer. When the brain slows down it takes the body down with it. We now know the brain holds the secret to how we age. Speed looks better, feels better, is better.

It's All in Your Mind

It would be impossible to write a book about the brain without addressing the subject of the mind. Of course, even broaching the subject could mean initiating a discussion to which there is no end. Debates about whether the brain is more important than the mind, or the mind is more important than the brain, or the mind and the brain are one and the same have been raging since the beginning of time. They are not going to be resolved here.

Nevertheless, it is a fact the mind has power over the brain, yet at the same time is somewhat unaware of the brain's needs. Brain maintenance is not considered on-the-job training when you are born. Brain 101 is not taught in school. So the mind never really learns how to nourish and nurture the brain. As a result the mind can develop some very bad habits where the brain is concerned. Who orders that sixth soda, that third candy bar, that pack of cigarettes, that one last drink? It is not brain, that's for sure. It's mind. After all, mind wants what mind wants, when it wants it, whether it is good for brain or not.

Mind tends to be demanding when it comes to brain. When brain is fatigued, foggy, or frazzled because it has been struggling at work all day, it is not brain that is up worried, afraid, and anxious all night. It is mind. Mind's attitude is that brain's work is never done. You never hear mind saying, "Oh brain, I'm sorry. I pushed you way past your limits. It is my fault that you can't even focus on what is right in front of you." Never. Mind likes to get away with murder. And it will, if you let it.

The truth is mind's connection with brain is incredibly important. Some days it seems like they are totally connected. Others, like the morning after the night before, brain won't have anything to do with mind. There is a reason. Brain's not getting enough of what it needs, and its getting way too much of what it doesn't need.

Your brain has been evolutionarily bred, groomed, and finely tuned for a lifetime of incredible service. This is its natural state. Optimal brain health and fitness are your birthright. But, in order to perform, your brain must have its three essential needs fully satisfied on a regular basis. Just like you, for optimal health and performance, your brain needs exercise, nourishment and rest — every day.

Brain Health and Fitness Training

Even though premature mental decline and mild cognitive impairment appear to be reaching nearly epidemic proportions, they are probably preventable and even reversible. Anyone, no matter what age, can learn faster, remember better, sustain focus longer, think and react quicker, boost problem-solving ability, enhance creativity and intuition, and make quicker, better decisions (choices). You can regenerate your brain, recharge your mind, and increase your brainpower, for life. All you have to do is meet your brain's three essential neural needs, neuro-nutrition, neuro-stimulation and neuro-rest and relaxation (R&R), every day.

Figures 2.2 and 2.3 illustrate two sets of data about brain speed. Figure 2.2 shows the age-related decline in processing speed as we age. Figure 2.3 demonstrates the brainpower (speed) improvement derived from a series of brain speed exercise sessions (participants typically did two five- to 10-minute sessions a day).

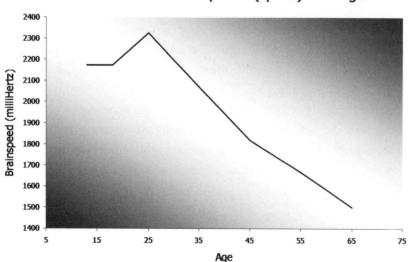

Natural Decline in Brainpower (speed) with Age

Figure 2.2*

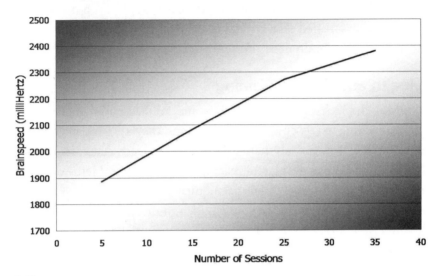

Increases in Brainpower (speed) with Brain Exercises

Figure 2.3*

As you can see from the graphs, brain speed exercises can lead to a profound upgrade in processing speed in less than 40 sessions (or 20 days if you are doing two a day). To witness this kind of improvement in muscle power it would take many hours of effort at the gym every week, for more than three to six months.

When you perform challenging brain speed exercises as quickly as possible, it fires up your brain cells. The stimulation that comes from interactive brain speed exercising forces brain cells in specific areas of your brain to work faster and communicate better. Learning, calculating, deciding, reacting, and remembering are all enhanced. Brain speed exercises help your brain grow new synapses and connections (dendrites and axons) and increase its processing speed. They put your brain in a high-performance mode, fast. In fact, brain speed exercise can create a unique experience of neural thrills and cerebral rushes unlike anything you have ever felt before.

Increasing Brain Speed

When it comes to your body, the physical results from exercise go up exponentially when resistance training is combined with the nutritional support of muscle-building supplements. Anyone can improve his or her physical strength, flexibility, and power with weight training combined with the right nutrients. The same holds true for the brain. If you want to increase your brain speed, and protect and support your brain right now, you can. All you have to do is give your brain the care it needs and it will respond by moving into a higher, healthier, more productive gear in just three weeks.

A well-intentioned and informed mind can develop and maintain high-level brainpower and speed. Your brain can be stimulated to develop remarkable new powers when you meet its basic needs. The purpose of this book is to teach you how to do that. I want you to learn how to treat your brain like it is your best friend, because it is. When you make friends with someone, you first have to get to know him or her. That is exactly what you are going to do with your brain, you are going to get to know it – what it is made of, how it works, and how the choices you make each day affect it. In the next chapter we are going to take a brief look at the physiology of your beautiful, beautiful brain.

---

* The source for figures 2.1, 2.2 and 2.3 is from presentations; "Speed of processing, the missing measure in early detection of MCI?", presented at the FDA Conference on Mild Cognitive Impairment (http://www.fda.gov/ohrms/dockets/ac/01/slides/3724s1_9_shah/), Mar 2002, and Longevity & Preventative Medicine Symposium 2002, Jan. '02, Tempe, AZ.

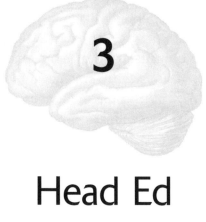

Head Ed

"Not only our pleasure, our joy and our laughter but also our sorrow, our pain, grief and tears arise from the brain, and the brain alone."

Hippocrates

Weighing in at approximately three pounds, or about two percent of your body weight, your brain is a living, breathing organ that is very demanding. At times, it can require over 20 percent of your oxygen intake and as much as 50 percent of the sugar circulating in your bloodstream in order to control your breathing, reproduction, digestion and elimination, and regulate your heartbeat, blood pressure, temperature, movement and reflexes, eating, drinking and thinking.

This is not a textbook, and I am not going to give you a complete course in the anatomy or function of the brain. But, I do believe the more you understand your amazing brain and how it works, the more you will marvel at its seemingly infinite capabilities and the more you will want to protect and take care of it.

Something Old

Brain science teaches that our brains evolved in three stages over millions of years. The first stage, sometimes called the old brain, can be traced back to what are believed to be our reptilian ancestors. This part of the brain is responsible for our basic instincts, and for regulating our heartbeats, breathing, and other automatic bodily processes. It also acts as a switchboard for the sensory data from our environment, feeding back instructions to the appropriate part of our brain when action is called for. Balance and movement through time and space are coordinated here. When you climb out of the pool, dry off with a towel, and then navigate your way to the bathhouse to change clothes, your reptilian brain is what gets you there.

The second stage in the evolution of the brain was the mammalian or mid-brain. Stacked on top of the old, instinctive, reptilian brain the mid-brain houses the amygdala, hippocampus, and hypothalamus. Together they are responsible for emotions, learning, and memory, and just about all of the hormonal activity going on in your body.

The amygdala monitors your world for threats and registers fear. It is involved in the formation of new memories, especially those that have strong emotional content — the more powerful the emotion, the longer and stronger the memory. Most of us will never forget the conditions surrounding our first awareness of the September 11, 2001 terrorist attack on the World Trade Center in New York City. Emotionally loaded memories like those associated with 9/11 become indelibly inked in our minds. Yet, if we are asked what we had for lunch yesterday, most of us have to stop and think hard about it. And, no matter how long we think about it many of us won't remember. It just wasn't important enough.

The hypothalamus gland plays a role in the rise and fall of your emotions, everything from love and hate to apathy and rage. It is also involved in regulating your hormone activity. For example, the hypothalamus gland helps your body determine how to respond to various stressors such as heat, cold, thirst, hunger, lust, and even fear. If a barking dog aggressively lunges toward you it is your hypothalamus that orders up the extra adrenaline you need to run away.

The hippocampus is the memory center of the brain, where short-term memories are processed and converted into long-term memories, and stored in the various nooks and crannies of your cerebral cortex. When the hippocampus is damaged a person may be forced to live in the past, able to recall experiences that happened long ago, but not able to remember something that happened yesterday. The hippocampus is located right behind the olfactory bulbs that govern what you can smell. Neurodegenerative diseases that start their hideous invasion of the brain in the hippocampus often knock out one's sense of smell. Loss of smell can signal the onset of early stage Alzheimer's disease.

Something New

The newest, and perhaps most important stage in the evolution of the brain is the cerebral cortex, also referred to as the cerebrum. The cerebral cortex looks almost like the bark on a tree stump. It is divided into a frontal cortex (or lobe), a temporal cortex, a parietal lobe, and an occipital cortex. Each lobe, or cortex, has its own functions. For example, the frontal and temporal lobes think, learn, remember, and generate self-awareness. The parietal lobe helps orient you in space and mark the distinction between you and the world around you. The occipital lobe controls seeing, visual memories, and other visual processes.

Science tells us that our cerebral cortex is split – that we have a left and a right brain. Left-brain activity includes language, logical reasoning, arithmetic, memory for words, writing skills, and scientific understanding. Right-brain activity includes spatial orientation and memory. For example, finding your way home, as well as music and art skills and appreciation, intuition and possibly imagination are all governed by the right brain. To say that you are either left or right brained can be misleading. You are actually both, except one side is generally more developed and dominant than the other.

Composed of hundreds of structures — lobes, cortexes, hemispheres, glands, and over 400 miles of capillaries — your brain is a very complex organ. What makes it all work? Billions of brain cells all communicating with each other, all of the time.

Your Brain is Electric

Your thoughts, memories, and feelings move through your brain as pulses of electrical signals, or messages. It has been estimated that there is enough electrical current running through your brain to light up a 25-watt lightbulb. Working somewhat like the relay system on a string of Christmas lights, these messages are passed from one neuron (brain cell) to another, through an intricate system called your neural network. This network forms the pathways that the messages move along until they reach their goal. Neurons actually look a little like lightbulbs.

Thoughts are a little like surfers riding along on the electro-chemical waves of your brain. Messages enter your brain cells through dendrites. Dendrites shuttle them into the neuron's cell body on a wave of electrical current. They cross the cell body and exit the neuron through the axons, which function somewhat like coaxial cables used in electronics. At the end of the axon is a synapse, a space or gap that exists between the transmitting neuron's axon and the receiving neuron's dendrite. To get from one synapse to another the messages are transported by neurotransmitters, chemicals that move them across the gap. This triggers another electrical signal that carries the message into the next dendrite and on to the next axon.

What is amazing about axons and dendrites, collectively known as neurites, is that your brain uses them to rewire and reconfigure itself when it is injured. This is the basis of what is called neuro-plasticity. If, for example, you have a stroke, head injury, or a concussion your brain has the remarkable ability to work around the injury by sprouting new neurites around the damaged or dying areas. Even more remarkable is that in a person who lost sight, the part of the brain responsible for seeing begins to network with other parts of the brain to compensate for the lost vision. Soon the cells of the occipital (vision) cortex are involved in actually enhancing other senses, such as hearing.

Your neural network connects all of the parts of your brain with each other, and with your body. If there is a breakdown anywhere along the network thoughts cannot get to their destinations quite as quickly or accurately. You might have a sense that you have a memory of something but you are unable to recall it. Or, you know there is a word for something you are trying to say, you just cannot access it. The health and fitness of your neural network determines the processing speed and efficiency of your mental processes.

Perhaps you have seen, or even known, someone who is considered slow. They are not generally slow in the realm of mobility, heart rate, or metabolism, but rather in mental performance. This can be because their brain processing speed is slow. Processing speed determines how quickly and efficiently new information can be learned, memories can be accessed, problems solved, decisions made, and actions taken. It determines brainpower and IQ, and new studies show it is even correlated with health and longevity.

Essentially Fat

Your brain is over 60 percent fat. But, this is not ordinary fat like the kind you find on a slab of beef. Your brain is made up of cholesterol, saturated fat, and two types of polyunsaturated fats, the Omega-3 and Omega-6 essential fatty acids. Every brain cell, or neuron, in your neural network is contained within a lipid membrane, or matrix, composed of important and highly specific ratios of all of these fats, and specific proteins.

This membrane balances and controls your brain cells' structural flexibility, integrity, and the all-important electrical characteristics needed to optimize its health, your mental performance capacity, and even your emotions. The phospholipid construction of your brain cell membrane, including its cholesterol level, gives it the fluidity it needs to pump vital nutrients into each cell, waste products out, and energy and information between cells, quickly. This membrane also acts as a master switch, facilitating the cellular communication necessary for thoughts and memories.

In order to function properly, neural membranes must have high structural integrity and flexibility with minimal stiffness, or rigidity. They must be permeable enough to allow nourishment in, but not so porous they leak energy out, causing cells to lose their vital life forces. When the membrane is compromised in any way the brain's ability to function begins to diminish.

Docosahexaenoic acid (DHA), an Omega-3 fatty acid, which is also found in fish oil, makes up almost 50 percent of the total fat content in your neural membranes. DHA forms the all-important building blocks, or bricks, of a brain cell's membrane. Your first encounter with DHA is in your mother's womb. Mother's milk is also loaded with DHA. Interestingly, low prenatal and breast-milk levels of DHA, as well as choline, in a mother can result in lower IQs and more cognitive impairment later in life for her child. In addition, studies have indicated that a DHA-rich childhood may protect against noninsulin dependent or adult onset diabetes, obesity, hypertension, and other diseases associated with impaired glucose metabolism.

Your brain loves fat, so much so that it will absorb virtually any type of fat, good or bad that you put into your stomach. And, therein lies a problem. For example, Arachidonic acid (AA) is an Omega-6 fatty acid that is also an important part of the lipid membrane, especially early in brain development. A balance between AA and DHA is mandatory for brain health and fitness as we age. When too much saturated fat or too many commercial polyunsaturated oils are present in the diet AA is produced in abundance, which throws the all-important DHA-to-AA ratio out of balance. Too much AA can inflame the brain, and accelerate the loss of brainpower.

When the fats in your diet lack sufficient membrane-building ingredients, or your fat intake comes primarily from processed foods and oils, your brain membranes can become faulty, somewhat like leaky gaskets in a car engine. If the head gasket in your engine is leaking, horsepower and performance start to sputter and decline. Eventually the engine burns out. The same is true for your brain. When your neural membranes are compromised, brainpower and brain health suffer.

Your diet can nourish or compromise your brain's membranes. When you have enough of the all-important essential brain-building fats in your diet, your brain can continually renew and rebuild its neurons. This improves brain speed, mental acuity, intelligence, memory, problem solving, language skills, and overall cognitive performance. You will learn much more about how to feed your brain in Chapters 8 and 9.

The Mighty Mitochondria

Inside each neuron are tiny energy generating powerhouses called the mitochondria. The mitochondria are the little internal combustion engines of cellular metabolism that provide the energy your brain needs for clear thinking, paying attention, remembering, and acting willfully. The health, tone, and fitness of your mitochondria and membranes determine your brain's speed, memory, processing power, and longevity.

Metabolically, your brain's mitochondria are very, very active. Even when you are sleeping they are hard at work. They are constantly generating energy for you and your brain cells. The energy efficiency of your little mitochondrial engines is up to 10 times more efficient then the high-tech engine powering your car. The hydrogen-oxygen fuel cells used in spacecraft are even less energy efficient. The source of life and death for neurons (and your brain) lies in your mighty, high functioning mitochondria.

Cognitive Currency

The basic chemical currency of energy exchange between all the cells in your brain and body is adenosine triphosphate, or ATP. The food we eat is oxidized to produce high-energy electrons that are then converted to ATP by your mitochondria. Any disruption in brain ATP activity can result in lower brain energy and, consequently, less mental clarity, focus, energy, and processing speed.

The mitochondria can easily develop flaws as we age. Poor brain nutrition is a major cause, as are infections, inflammation, free radicals, neurotoxic pollutants, and stress. Excess cortisol, your stress hormone, is very hard on the mighty mitochondria. As mitochondrial defects accumulate, they cause increasing dysfunction: reduced ATP production, compromised cellular energy, increased free radical generation and inflammation, and ultimately increased cell death. Mental acuity, energy, and memory all suffer. If the process continues, at a certain threshold trigger point neurodegenerative disease sets in. Scientists now believe that even Alzheimer's disease may stem from a continuous process of membrane and mitochondrial breakdown over a long period of time.

Fuel for Thought

Your brain cells crave sugar, or blood glucose. They love the energy that comes with a sugar rush. The mitochondria use glucose, as well as fatty acids to make energy. Under normal conditions your brain uses up to 25 percent of the sugar circulating in your bloodstream to fuel its mighty mitochondria. In moments of peak mental performance your brain can devour up to half the sugar in your blood. Remember, it weighs only two percent of the body's weight. What a sugar-hungry glutton the brain is.

Normally you have the equivalent of one teaspoon of sugar circulating in your bloodstream. You also have a certain level of insulin in your bloodstream, which helps your body utilize the circulating sugar efficiently and stay metabolically active. But the relationship between insulin and blood sugar is a delicate balance, easily altered when you flood your system with the extra glucose that comes from eating too many sweets or starchy, high-glycemic carbohydrates.

When your brain calculates sugar overload it demands more insulin so the sugar can be utilized by the brain cells, or metabolized and removed from the bloodstream. However, if too much insulin is pumped into the system blood sugar levels crash and you find yourself experiencing a good case of the sugar blues — low mental energy and high brain fuzz. Thus, a vicious cycle can begin that puts your brain in a kind of chronic stress mode.

When brain glucose levels seesaw you can experience a dramatic change in brain energy that wipes out concentration, mental clarity, and productivity. In addition, excess insulin can cause a rise in dangerous free radical levels and damage the delicate inner linings of the cerebral capillary walls. It may even scorch sensitive brain cell membranes. In fact, longevity scientists now believe uncontrolled surges or sustained high levels of insulin can be one of the major accelerators of aging.

Thinking Machine

Remarkably, even when you think about your brain you are using your brain to do it. But, your brain does much more than just think. It learns, calculates, and directs. It determines your mood, your disposition, your memories, and all of your choices. It coordinates, controls, and contemplates. It decides what goes on in your body, and how you manage what goes on in your life. Your brain unites the various parts of yourself with each other: your heart and lungs with your bones and muscles; your stomach, liver, and pancreas with your kidneys and colon; your endocrine system with your digestion and metabolism. Your brain connects you with all the aspects of your life: the world you live in, your family and friends, community, job, and society. It tells you how to react to situations and respond to questions.

Your brain also sees, listens, feels, smells, tastes, and speaks. It remembers, creates, analyzes, and concludes. It computes, imagines, concentrates, ignores, sleeps, dreams, draws, reads, and writes. And if that is not enough, it does all of this in an environment that is constantly changing. So, how does it do all of this? In the next chapter we are going to take a closer look at how your amazing brain does what it does.

4

You Have More Brains Than You Think

"The real voyage of discovery consists not in seeking new lands,
but in seeing with new eyes."

Marcel Proust

For the purpose of this book, and to help you better grasp how your high-performance brain engine works, I am going to use a four-brain model. I want you to envision that you have four brains, or brain systems, all working together to manage the miracle that is you. You have a sensory and motor brain (S&M), an attention and thinking brain (A&T), a learning and memory brain (L&M), and a feeling and emoting brain (F&E). They function somewhat like networked computers, each with its own processing center. The speed with which they process information and communicate with each other is what determines how well you feel and function in your life. The image in Figure 4.1 represents where these processing centers are located in your brain.

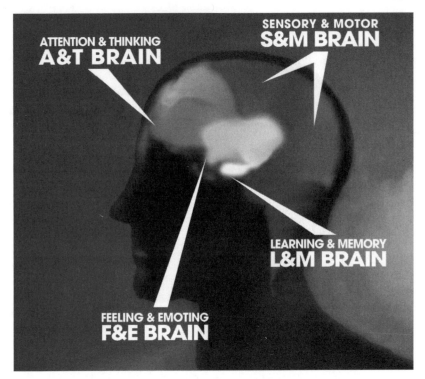

Figure 4.1. The relative locations of the processing centers in your brain.

Your Sentient Brain

You perceive and react to your world via your sensory and motor (S&M) brain. Most of its activities are relatively automatic. For example, imagine you are in the kitchen tossing a salad and someone comes in and distracts you. As you turn to speak to the person you knock the salad bowl off the counter. Without hesitation you grab the bowl in midair, preventing it from crashing to the floor. You don't have to think about it, you just do it. That is if your S&M brain is able to take in the necessary information, process it, formulate an action plan, and then carry it out swiftly enough. If it isn't, the salad bowl is likely to hit the floor and you will have to come up with something different for lunch.

Your attention and thinking (A&T) brain, scientifically known as working memory, is the executive center — the planning, organizing, problem-solving, decision-making, and take-action part of your brain. Without your A&T brain you would not only be unable to organize your closets, you would also be incapable of organizing your thoughts. Your A&T brain is responsible for directing and holding your attention, for split-second decisions as well as long, thought-out logic, reasoning, and problem solving. Many believe it is not only the center of your intelligence but that it is also the seat of your consciousness and self-awareness.

If you are in your car speeding along a winding road and suddenly you are faced with an intersection and a big yellow traffic light, what do you do? You either speed up to make the light, or you slam on your brakes so you can stop before the light turns red. A split-second decision or choice is made. In this case, and in similar situations, the right decision is made quite easily if your A&T brain is processing all the information it needs quickly and efficiently.

As you are reading this paragraph, if your intention is to learn and remember it, then you are activating your learning and memory (L&M) brain. The level of interest or consideration your A&T brain places on newly registered information determines how successfully your L&M brain will accurately file away the information for storage. What many people fear as serious memory loss may in reality be fading or fickle powers of attention.

Working like a switchboard, your L&M brain shuttles newly learned and old retrieved information back and forth between your A&T brain and the widespread stores of memory throughout your cerebral cortex. The availability of your more recent memories — what you had for lunch yesterday, names of people you met recently, who you were with at the last movie you saw, or items you wrote on a shopping list – all depend on how quickly information gets processed by your L&M brain.

Your feeling and emoting (F&E) brain also plays a very important role in how well memories are stored, and how quickly and easily they are retrieved. Our keenest memories are often those that are formed during a powerful surge of emotion. Most people, for instance, will never forget their first kiss, or what they were doing when they learned of the death of Princess Diana.

Memories Are Made Of This

The more we learn about memory the more we discover that there are many forms. Many associated and seemingly inseparable memories such as the color, fabric, and design of your wedding dress and the chapel you were married in are all stored in vastly different areas of the brain.

We have all had the experience of running into a person we recognize, maybe we have even had a sense of where we knew the person from, but were unable to remember the person's name in that moment. This is the result of the brain's inability to quickly seek out and retrieve each associated component of the memory, efficiently organize what it has retrieved, and present it to the conscious, considering A&T executive brain.

Memory, then, depends on your intention and commitment to remembering. It also depends on your attention and thinking brain's connection with your learning and memory brain, the health and fitness of both brains and, of course, the speed of communication among them. The added energy of emotion, regardless of whether it is positive or negative, also improves the imprint of the memory, making it easier to retrieve later.

Interestingly, the final stage in the formation of a long-term memory happens when you are sleeping. It is now believed that what is learned, or properly encoded and consolidated by your attention and thinking brain, and stored away by your learning and memory brain, can only become a permanent memory through a process called long-term potentiation (LTP).

LTP occurs during the stage of deep sleep known as slow-wave sleep. It may also occur during rapid-eye movement or REM sleep, when dreaming takes place. As we age, the amount of time we spend in slow-wave sleep (the most stress-releasing state of sleep) and REM steeply declines. This is due to a natural, age-related increase in the stress hormone cortisol, as well as other biochemical changes brought on by excess stress, poor food choices, an overactive mind, and lower levels of stress-reducing serotonin. Shortened, interrupted sleep, and compromised slow-wave sleep and REM reduce the effectiveness of LTP, leading to poor recall of recently learned information. Interestingly, this can also happen when we are younger if kids, neighbors, pets, stress, or an overactive, chattering mind disturb our sleep.

Your F&E brain isn't just responsible for your feelings and emotions. It is also in charge in large part of your hormone production, and the regulation of your body's response to stress. When stress hormone levels are elevated, REM sleep is shortened. Studies involving college students found that when their REM sleep was reduced, such as when they pulled an all-nighter to study for finals, their memory capacity for learned material was much poorer the next day than that of students who had gotten a full night's sleep. Deep, restful sleep is very important for a good memory.

Your Brain on Hormones

Your endocrine system and hormones have been described as your body's great information superhighway. Together they manage and control everything from your energy expenditures to how well your immune system is working. Your endocrine system is comprised of the glands that produce your hormones, the chemical messengers that relay information back and forth between your brain, and the various parts of your body. A complex partnership known as the hypothalamus-pituitary-adrenal axis, or HPA, forms the cornerstone of this communication network. Together the hypothalamus and pituitary glands function like hormonal traffic cops, regulating and controlling your body's hormone production, and insuring balanced and healthy body and brain function.

Here is an example of how it works. Your sensory and motor brain perceives an external threat to your safety – this could be anything from a horrendously turbulent ride on an airplane to a snarling dog headed your way. Or, your attention and thinking brain could be obsessed with an imagined threat, a negative thought, or a situation that invokes anxiety or fear. Maybe you have just had a very restless night's sleep. Or, your body has been subjected to intense physical stress or trauma, such as extreme cold or a burn, even a microorganism or virus entering your body and wreaking havoc with your immune system. The point here is that something stressful happens, and when it does your sensory and motor brain sends up a flare that tells your feeling and emoting brain to activate its fight or flight mechanism. This results in a signal from your hypothalamus to your adrenal gland to crank up the production of your stress hormones, cortisol and adrenaline (epinephrine).

The ensuing rush of hormones elevates your blood pressure and heart rate, re-routes and increases blood flow to your brain and central nervous system, and increases your blood sugar for energy. Now you are ready to run away, face the enemy and do battle, or simply cope with the stressor. Once the stressful situation has been dealt with, your feeling and emoting brain, in concert with the HPA, shuts down the stress response so your body can recover and begin functioning normally again. Ideally, cortisol and adrenaline levels return to normal, and your body calms down. Unfortunately, as you age, and as your brain accumulates the effects of chronic stress, the HPA pathways get frayed and the glands get worn down. The HPA loses its ability to turn off the stress response. Cortisol keeps flooding into your brain cells. Too much cortisol in the brain over an extended period of time can be very damaging to brain cells. You will learn more about this in Chapter 5.

Another hormone that affects your brain, mood, and memory is DHEA. DHEA is an anti-stress hormone that buffers the effects of cortisol and also stimulates brain function. As you age the adrenals start producing less and less DHEA, resulting in less protection against the brain-ravaging effects of stress.

Incidentally, when you are in an emotional situation, such as fear or passion, the temperature of your entire body, or even just parts of it, can change. The expressions "cold with fear" and "hot with passion" reflect what happens in the body when the sympathetic and parasympathetic nervous systems are activated by emotion via the F&E (feeling and emoting brain). In response to emotions these systems regulate bodily functions, such as increasing blood flow and warming us up when we are stimulated or aroused by passion. This psychological-physiological response was actually the basis for my stress card and the Mood Ring.

Quick Draw McGraw

Your sensory and motor brain's processing speed is known in psychology as simple, or physical, reaction time, and it is measured in a few hundred milliseconds, which is a few tenth's of a second. Physical reaction time is known as a subcortical response since it involves little or no cognitive processing, only pure sensory-motor information registration and action. The average fit and healthy sensory motor brain can respond to a stimulus in a mere 250 to 300 milliseconds (reaction time). When you are driving that is just about how long it takes your S&M brain to register and identify a red light and send a command to your leg to apply the brakes. It all happens in about _ of a second.

Now, remember the bend in the road and the yellow light driving example mentioned earlier? Your response in that situation involved a split-second decision, or choice – whether to stop or accelerate through the light. In a fit and healthy attention and thinking brain it generally takes 400 to 500 milliseconds to make this kind of split-second decision. Since thinking about what to do would take a second or longer, your potentially lifesaving decision is made considerably faster than if you had to stop and think about it. In fact, you are smarter (quicker) than you can think.

Now suppose there was a more challenging decision you had to make. Let's say you are traveling fairly fast and when you round the bend the light appears. What if something else unexpected happens? What if there is a car coming into the intersection on your right and the driver of that car is also deciding whether to stop or time the light and keep going? Now you have a complex decision to make, with more variables to compute. But again you make it almost effortlessly in just a fraction of a second. Why? Because your reaction time for making a complex decision is still less than a second (typically 500 to 1,000 milliseconds depending on the complexity and number of choices involved). This is your brain's processing speed when it is under a heavy load, or challenge. Your life or death choice is still made faster than the time it takes to stop and think about it.

Put into the context of our yellow light example, the faster your reaction time the quicker you will be able to stop. A person with the reaction time of a 20-year-old would have 33 more feet to maneuver than a person with the reaction time of a 45-year-old. That means if the decision to stop placed the faster person 10 feet short of the intersection, the slower person would overshoot it by 23 feet and possibly cause a serious accident.

Luckily, a steep decline in brain speed is not inevitable, and it is definitely reversible. Just like the processing speed in your computer can be upgraded, your brain's processing speed can be increased, dramatically. Someone older can improve his or her mental processing powers to equal, and even exceed, that of a much younger person. Your brain speed and efficiency depend on the biochemistry, health, and fitness of your brain cells.

Unfortunately, most of us have never learned about brain cell maintenance, let alone brain building. In addition, keeping our brains healthy and fit is not something many of us have given much thought to. Most of us just seem to take our brains for granted. But consider this, neuroscience now knows that like the body, the brain is very vulnerable, actually more vulnerable, to the environment we live in, the foods we eat, and the amount of stress, rest, and relaxation we experience.

High Performance

Your high-performance brain is always at work. Even when you are sleeping your hyperactive little neurons keep chug, chug, chugging away, providing the energy your brain needs to regulate your bodily functions, as well as to dream and to work out the residual stresses of the day. If you look at the brain symbolically, and compare it to a high-performance engine, then you could say its tachometer is running close to red line most of the time. Your brain's work is never done.

In the same way that a high-performance engine requires constant vigilance and maintenance, so does your brain. A little imbalance in the timing, a tiny speck of dirt in the fuel lines, or a low-octane fuel can all throw an engine's performance out of whack. Well, remember those 400 miles of brain capillaries that are constantly providing passage for the oxygen, glucose, and other nutrients to reach your brain cells? They are so narrow that even the minutest lesion, amount of plaque, or spot of inflammation can form a destructive obstruction to the nourishing and protecting flow of nutrients your brain needs in order to thrive, if not survive.

In the next chapter I am going to focus on the delicate biochemistry of the brain, what can destroy precious brain cells, and cause the significant loss in brainpower many of us are experiencing by the time we are in our prime. As difficult as the chapter may be to read, I hold to those old adages, "knowledge is power," and "forewarned is forearmed." It is only after you recognize the enemy that you can formulate an effective campaign against it.

Don't worry; it is not all bad news. We are in the midst of a neurological crisis, it is true. But, the solutions necessary to change the tide are rapidly emerging. Every day we are learning that it is almost never too late to improve brain health and fitness. It all depends on your willingness to improve your brain care habits and your commitment to fulfilling your brain's vital daily needs.

5

Your Vulnerable Brain

"It is possible that in changing the way we view a thing,
we may actually change the thing viewed."

Joseph C. Pearce

The Industrial Revolution has been a pain to your brain. I call it modern-day brain pain. With our advancement into modern times has come more and more pollution everywhere — in our air, food, and water. Is there any doubt that lead has a negative impact on the brain? Not anymore. But lead is not our only problem.

Aluminum exposure has been linked to Alzheimer's disease. It has been found in high concentrations in the beta amyloid plaques of people diagnosed with Alzheimer's. We have polychlorinated biphenyls (PCBs) in our landfills and all along the food chain. PCBs are carcinogens that also have a negative impact on our immune, reproductive, nervous, and endocrine systems. We have mercury in our fish, and in our teeth. Mercury exposure has been indicated in the formation of neurofibrillary tangles and amyloid plaques, two indicators of Alzheimer's disease.

Xenoestrogens, or synthetic estrogens, are also permeating our environment. They can be found in everything from plastics to pesticides to the food we eat. In the body xenoestrogens bind with estrogen receptor cells, preventing natural estrogen from binding, thus blocking its normal function. In addition, they can enter the nucleus of a receptor cell and disrupt cell growth and division. Birds exposed to xenoestrogens experience reproductive failure, growth retardation, life-threatening deformities, and brain and liver dysfunction.

There are other neural insults besides pollutants and heavy metals. Bacteria, viruses, funguses, and injuries can all be detrimental to the brain. The initial inflammation that comes with any one of these insults often triggers a cascade of events resulting in neuronal compromise and loss, premature mental decline, and eventually even Alzheimer's. In fact, inflammation can be both the initial triggering event and the final death blow to your vulnerable neurons.

When you catch a cold your body's immune system responds by turning up your body temperature in an attempt to kill the viral or bacterial invader. This healthy inflammatory process soon subsides, invaders retreat, and the body is well again. Usually. Unfortunately, as we age this natural immune response can linger on as chronic, low-grade, or smoldering inflammation. It becomes self-perpetuating, but below our normal level of awareness. Over time this can trigger a cascade of destructive events in the brain. Many now believe that most forms of dementia, including Alzheimer's disease, are the result of brain inflammation. This is why anti-inflammatory pills, such as ibuprofen, have been shown to lower the risk of Alzheimer's.

Cumulative Damage

Unfortunately, the negative effects of brain stressors are cumulative, which means that even our sins of the past can render us more vulnerable to premature mental decline, MCI, and Alzheimer's. For example, maybe you partied and drank quite a bit when you were young. But now, you just drink and party socially. Studies show that binge drinking when you were in your teens and early 20s can exact their toll when you reach middle age. This manifests as forgetfulness, foggy thinking, and fumbling for names, words, and memories.

We now know that fast-food diets during teenage years can result in insulin resistance when you are older. Insulin resistance is the body's inability to respond to the insulin it produces. It can lead to glucose intolerance, diabetes, obesity, and heart disease, and it can seriously downgrade brainpower.

Head injuries or blows to the head when you are young can also take their toll on your brain much later in life. And that is not just from serious concussions, it can be the kind of steady tap, tap, tapping that comes with heading the ball in soccer. One study in the United Kingdom revealed that after age 40 club soccer players have pronounced memory deficits compared to others their age.

When we are young we don't generally notice any decline in our cognitive capacity because we have reserves, extra neural connections and brain cells that provide backup power when we need it. But as we age, the reserves seem to diminish quickly. Consequently, with even the slightest insult – a little fatigue, insomnia, jet lag, a hangover, or a cold — we can feel forgetful, spacey, foggy, or fuzzy in the head. Those extra connections seem to have disappeared, just when we need them most.

Anatomy of a Killer

Science has long known that continual stress weakens the immune system and puts us at risk for chronic, degenerative disease. However, one of the most chilling scientific discoveries of recent times revealed that the daily stress most of us experience may be killing our brain cells.

Stress is necessary. In fact, it can be good for you. It can challenge your body, mind, and soul. It can drive you, motivate you, even help you accomplish your goals. Life just would not be life without a little stress.

Many of us think of stress as something big and eventful, such as the death of a loved one, a divorce, a bankruptcy, or an auto accident. But worry, fear, anger, and resentment cause stress. Jobs, relationships, and changes cause stress. All forms of stress can hurt the brain; however, of all the stress factors that affect your highly vulnerable brain none harms it more than chronic stress.

In your body, stress is a hormonal event that is designed to save your life. Cortisol, your stress hormone, is a key player in your fight or flight response. Under normal conditions cortisol helps regulate blood pressure, mineral and electrolyte balance, and the breakdown and utilization of proteins, carbohydrates, and fats. It is necessary for fighting inflammation, for the mobilization of glucose and fatty acids in the bloodstream, and a host of other important physiological functions.

When you are experiencing stress, cortisol triggers the release of sugar into your bloodstream to increase your energy and strength. When you are under the gun (pressure to think or perform fast) cortisol also has a powerful influence on your brain, sharpening your senses, and heightening your ability to gather and process information more quickly.

However, cortisol also has a dark side. Under the influence of chronic, unrelenting stress, or as a result of aging, the brain's cortisol-regulating mechanism can break down, sending cortisol production spiraling out of control. We now know that continually elevated cortisol levels can seriously put your brain at risk. Studies show that patients under severe long-term stress have lost as much as 25 percent of their hippocampus, the learning and memory center of the brain. In much the same way that a blowout of one of the four tires on your car makes it nearly impossible to drive, losing a fourth of your hippocampus critically impairs brain performance and emotional well-being. First there is a subtle loss in mental quickness. Then powers of concentration, clarity, and memory start to fade. Once MCI (mild cognitive impairment) sets in, the door to Alzheimer's has been opened.

Costs of Chronic Stress

- Elevates cortisol, glucose, and blood pressure
- Impairs glucose uptake and metabolism
- Increase risk of insulin resistance
- Kills brain cells
- Prevents neurogenesis, the formation of new brain cells
- Reduces blood flow to brain
- Harms the mitochondria
- Increases lipid peroxidation, damaging delicate membranes
- Impairs memory, focus, and thinking
- Weakens the immune system
- Increases hormonal imbalance
- Sleep loss
- Depression

Chattering Minds

One of the biggest triggers of cortisol overload and rapid brain aging may be thinking. That is right; much of our daily thinking is actually stressful. It is also relatively unconscious. How often have you found yourself daydreaming, or trying to fall asleep, and then gradually becoming aware that there is a steady stream of mental chatter echoing somewhere in the back of your head? Your mind is at it again, it is thinking. Mind loves to hear itself think.

Chatter clutters up the mind. Messages moving from one part of the brain to another become clouded. That is when miscalculations, errors in judgment, and mistakes become more frequent, at work, at home, behind the wheel of your car. A noisy, chattering mind undermines your ability to make a decision. It distracts you, making concentration almost impossible, which can make it significantly harder to take in new information. All this noise diminishes your creativity, your ability to observe and learn, to properly file away new information and quickly retrieve it, and to think fast and act smart. It also shortens your attention span. But wait a minute, it's true that some days your mind feels all mushy and fuzzy, but some days it feels very clear and focused. Maybe mental chatter is something changeable. It is. You can quiet your noisy mind, clear your head, amplify subtle intuitive signals from within, and boost mental efficiency, all by managing your mental chatter. I am going to show you how in Chapter 11.

Techno-Stress

Of all the brain stressors, one of the worst is techno-stress — the incessant influx of new information we are confronted with each day and the accelerated rate of change we all have to live with day in and day out. Techno-stress is considered a primary cause of a growing number of health problems ranging from anxiety, depression, high blood pressure, and sleep disorders to Alzheimer's disease.

Never before in the history of the world has life changed so rapidly. Technology is developing at an explosive pace. The global community is shrinking. When something happens across the world we know about it within moments. We are exposed to local news, national news, and now world news every night. If the stock market in Japan takes a dive the market in New York responds almost immediately.

The Internet is growing exponentially, communication systems are developing so rapidly you can hardly keep up with the latest devices. We have cell phones that take photos, iPods™ that record and play music, Blackberries™ that organize your life – all inundating us with instruction manuals and more and more information to learn. Every year we are faced with an increase of several exabytes of new information. In computer talk an exabyte is a quintillion (one followed by 18 zeros) bytes of information. Now that is a lot of information. No wonder we are stressed out.

To keep up with this phenomenal expansion of information, computer processing speed has had to double almost every year. But, what about our poor brains? How are they coping with this relentless assault of new information? Have our brainpower and processing speeds been doubling annually? Actually, just the opposite seems to be happening. Continually having to process this torrential stream of data and new information is woefully straining our brains and our brainpower is suffering.

So, how is the stress level in your life? What does an average day look like for your brain? Here is a little quiz you can take to determine whether or not the stress in your life is affecting your brain.

Stress Quiz

1. Do you have to leave home early to get to work on time because you have to fight commuter traffic?
2. Is breakfast a cup of java and bagel, or a piece of toast? Or, do you skip breakfast entirely?
3. Do you feel the stress of having to keep up with younger coworkers who seem so techno-savvy, and mentally quick?
4. How about lunch? Do you grab for snacks, chips, or fill up on sweets?
5. When you get home are there more tasks and responsibilities waiting for your attention – bills, chores, and children?
6. Do you grab a high-fat, fast-food dinner, on the run?
7. When you finally do get to bed are all those chattering voices in your head keeping you awake?
8. Are you snoring more, smoking more, snacking more, drinking more, or vegging out more just so you can cope, and stay afloat?
9. Do you ever find yourself starting to say something, and forgetting

what it was, or walking into a room and forgetting why you are there?

10. When you are busy doing one thing is your mind preoccupied with something else, making it nearly impossible to concentrate on the task at hand?

So, if you answered yes to more than three of these questions your brain may be in overload. And overload is going to slow it down. Not to worry. There is something you can do about all of this stress.

Accentuate the Positive

One of the first steps in stress management is learning to recognize when stress is getting to you. Listen to your body — a racing heartbeat, rapid breathing, tense muscles, and sweaty palms or cold hands can all be symptoms that you are stressed, anxious, or in fear. A knot in your stomach, or a feeling of queasiness, dry mouth, and teeth clenching or grinding can also be signs that stress is getting the best of you. If you notice any of these symptoms, it may be time to give your brain a break, before it puts the brakes on your health and performance.

Take some time to do something you enjoy – every day. Put your worries on the back burner for a short time and allow yourself to have some fun. Get outside and move your body, take a walk in the sun, go for a swim or a bike ride. Spend time with a friend, laugh, treat yourself to a massage, visit a spa, and at the end of the day, get a good night's sleep.

Another antidote to brain stress is brain speed exercise, which may seem ironic. After all, your mind may already feel like it is speeding out of control. But, what do you do when your computer is overloaded with too much information to process and not enough memory to handle it? Upgrade its processor, of course. That way the computer can better manage its workload. And that is exactly what speed exercises can do for your brain – upgrade its processing speed to the speed of change.

Every Breath You Take

Oxygen is one of your brain's primary fuel sources. In fact, your brain demands up to 20 percent of your total oxygen intake. This is mighty gluttonous for an organ that weighs only two percent of your body weight. The blood circulating through your cerebral capillaries literally bathes your brain cells in oxygen. Without a continuous supply of oxygen brain cells die.

Nevertheless, when it comes to the brain, oxygen, like cortisol, also has a down side. It is called oxidative stress and it is caused by an excess of free radicals in your cells and bloodstream. A certain amount of free radical production in your body is necessary, even desirable. It can help fight infections, even kill off cancer cells. In excess, though, free radicals can be quite harmful to your brain.

Free radicals are molecules that are missing an electron, which renders them unstable. This instability makes them highly reactive. They circulate through the body searching for other healthy molecules that have electrons they can steal. This in turn can set off a chain reaction that damages delicate brain cells and harms the membranes and mitochondria.

The membrane surrounding your neurons and their little internal energy producers, the mitochondria, is called the lipid bilayer. It is comprised of saturated and polyunsaturated fats and the all-important Omega-3 essential fatty acid, DHA. Like most fats and oils, the lipid membrane in your brain is highly susceptible to peroxidation, a particularly damaging form of free radical attack. Excessive alcohol (acetylaldehyde), a diet containing bad brain fats and foods, and stress all expose your brain to unnecessarily high levels of free radicals. The effects of these free radicals on the delicate phospholipid membranes could be likened to the effect of pouring acid on your skin.

Go With the Flow

Your brain is a heavy breather. It likes plenty of clean, oxygen-rich and ionized air. Ions are invisible molecules that are odorless and tasteless. We breathe them in every day. Ions are created when air or water molecules are broken apart by movement, radiation, even sunlight. It is the negatively charged ions in air that give it freshness and energy. Think about the feeling of invigoration you get when you are at the ocean, in the mountains, sitting beside a roaring fire or near a waterfall – it's all those negative ions in the air that turn your brain on. In fact, some studies now show that negative ions can actually increase the flow of oxygen to the brain. Negative ions are also believed to help increase the production of serotonin, which can help reduce depression and stress, and boost energy. Unfortunately, many highly polluted urban areas have low levels of oxygen and negative ions, and high levels of neurotoxins in the air. Hermetically sealed modern office buildings that recirculate air are ion depleted.

Air smart is brain smart. Put plants in your work and home environment. Plants use carbon dioxide to manufacture and release oxygen into the air. Air ionizers can truly freshen and enliven the air in any room. Of course, no matter how clean your air is, you still have to get it to your brain. Increasing cerebral circulation is the only way to do that. Exercise is one of the best ways to increase circulation and oxygen flow to your brain. That's exercising your brain and your body. Aerobic exercise not only increases blood flow to the hippocampus, your learning and memory center, it can actually trigger the growth of new brain cells, a process called neurogenesis. It is also been shown to increase the amount of recently learned information you can retain.

Eliminate the Negative

The evils of fat where obesity and cardiovascular disease are concerned are widely recognized. However, it was recently revealed that overweight people have smaller hippocampus regions in their brains, similar to the atrophied hippocampus found in Alzheimer's sufferers. Any damage to your memory center, or L&M brain, of course, can seriously compromise your memory. Sixty-six percent of Americans are deemed overweight.

Obesity aside, most people are completely unaware of the effects certain fats have on the brain. Remember, your brain cell membranes are mostly fat. A significant amount of your brain's energy metabolism depends upon the health and fitness of those fatty little membranes. The fats in your diet can have a powerful influence on them.

The worst fats for your brain are trans fatty acids, or trans fats. When natural oils, like sunflower seed or corn oil, go through the industrial refining process known as hydrogenation their molecular structure is chemically altered — forever. These once-healthy molecules now act more like plastic polymers, especially in your bloodstream where they can attach themselves to capillary walls and membranes, and slow down intracellular communication.

Trans fats are found in everything from French fries, potato chips, and fried chicken to shortening and margarine. They are also hidden in virtually all baked goods from bagels and baguettes to cookies, cakes, pastries, and pretzels. Trans fats can easily be incorporated into your delicate neuronal membranes. Recent studies show that eating foods and snacks high in trans fat for a mere four weeks can significantly impair memory.

Next in the bad brain fat lineup are commercial vegetable oils commonly used for salads and cooking. These oils are also known as Omega-6, polyunsaturated, or linoleic acid oils. Unless their label states that they are cold pressed, they probably contain trans fatty acids as mentioned above. However, there is another reason they can be brain damaging, especially when you get too much of them from your diet. The brain needs a certain balance of Omega-6s (linoleic fatty acids) and Omega-3s (linolenic fatty acids) in order to remain fit and healthy. When this balance is out of kilter, with the Omega-6s in excess of the Omega-3s by more than a 3:1 ratio, the effect can be very damaging to brain cell membranes, and your memory.

Arachidonic acid (AA) is an essential fatty acid derived from meat. It is also synthesized in the body from the Omega-6 fats and oils. AA is a vital component of the lipid membrane, especially early in life when a fetus or newborn baby's brain is developing. As we age the membrane's balance between AA and DHA becomes very critical. An excess of AA increases inflammation in the brain and can accelerate brain aging. Unfortunately, the typical American diet is too rich in the Omega-6 polyunsaturated oils and too deficient in the brain-essential fatty acids DHA and EPA (from fish oil). This contributes to excess AA production and hence inflammation in the brain.

Inflammation has long been considered a necessary, maybe even a healthy, byproduct of infection or injury. However, now a host of degenerative diseases such as diabetes, cardiovascular disease, and Alzheimer's are believed to be caused, or at least exacerbated, by inflammatory processes. Some scientists believe that a significant percentage of people older than 40 suffer from a low-level, kind of chronic, smoldering brain inflammation. Excessive cortisol, insulin, and free radical production, as well as a disproportionate consumption of Omega-6 commercial oils and the resulting AA imbalance can all fan the flames of inflammation. Inflammation, regardless of its cause, leads to a vicious cycle of increased free radical production and more inflammation.

Factors That Lead to Brain Inflammation

- Acute, chronic, or low-grade smoldering infections — bacterial, viral, or fungal
- Head injury — concussion, whiplash, even sports-related repetetive blows
- Oxidative stress — increased free radicals
- Consumption of trans fats
- Chronically elevated glucose, insulin, and cortisol levels
- Inadequate antioxidant protection
- Environmental toxins — heavy metals, mercury, lead, pesticides, etc.
- Alcohol — binge and chronic drinking

Metabolic Syndrome, also known as Syndrome X, is a prediabetic condition characterized by three or more of any of the following conditions: high blood pressure, insulin resistance, abdominal obesity, elevated blood glucose or triglyceride levels, and low HDL, the good cholesterol. It is believed to affect up to 50 million Americans and has been associated with a higher-than-normal degree of cognitive impairment. However, the cognitive impairment is significant only when inflammation levels are above normal.

Last but certainly not least on the list of the bad fats for your brain are the long-chain saturated fats, predominantly found in animal and dairy products. The long-chain saturated fats from animal sources have not only been implicated in obesity, cardiovascular disease, insulin resistance, and diabetes, but also Alzheimer's, stroke, and other forms of vascular dementia. However, since these saturated animal fats come from meat typically high in AA, it is not clear if the saturated fat or the AA is the primary cognitive culprit. Butter, coconut oil, and a few other vegetable sources contain a healthy form of medium-chain, saturated fat.

Swing Low Sweet Carbohydrates

The brain needs sugar in order to function. That is a fact. When there is too little sugar (hypoglycemia) available, mental energy, focus, and productivity all suffer. But too much sugar can lead to glucose intolerance and insulin resistance and a seesaw of insulin and glucose surges that weaken delicate neural membranes, inflame cerebral capillaries, accelerate free radical degeneration, and ultimately pollute and restrict blood flow to the brain's thinking and memory center. The net results are the same – first comes suboptimal mental performance, then premature mental decline, then mild cognitive impairment. Then you have a brain, mind, and memory that are in serious trouble.

Eating foods that are high on the glycemic index is what sets the sugar insulin seesaw in motion. The glycemic index ranks carbohydrates according to the amount of time it takes them to convert to sugar in your blood after you have eaten them. The blood sugar effect of eating straight glucose establishes the reference score of 100. Any carbohydrate over 50 on the index is considered a high-glycemic carb. High-glycemic carbs raise glucose levels very quickly which, in turn, raises your insulin level significantly. Almost as soon as you consume high-glycemic carbohydrates, such as cookies, croissants, sodas, or even potatoes you experience a sugar rush, that sense of heightened energy and awareness we all love. Please see Table 8.1 in Chapter 8.

You can protect your brain and avoid insulin spikes and blood sugar crashes by maintaining a carbohydrate balance that is no more than 40 to 50 percent of your total caloric intake, and by eating carbohydrates that are low (below 50) on the glycemic index. Including fiber and some fat, such as olive oil in your meal, and supplementing your diet with chromium, a brain-precious trace mineral also known as glucose tolerance factor can also lower the carb impact. You will learn much more about this in Chapter 8.

One source of hidden blood sugar bombshells is alcohol. In the body, alcohol converts very rapidly into sugar. Plus, many drinks are high in carbohydrates. Beer, wine, and especially sweetened mixed drinks can trigger the glucose insulin seesaw. Alcohol can also damage the liver and impair its ability to detoxify or remove excess sugar and toxins from the blood. This is not good for your brain.

Pickles Your Brain

From time to time many of us use alcohol to relax and have a good time. We have a few drinks, lose a few inhibitions at social affairs, perk up the brain energy (for a short while), and a good time is had by all. New evidence even shows that small amounts of alcohol can have health benefits, such as raising the good cholesterol (HDL). Studies have also shown that several drinks a week might even lower one's risk of cognitive impairment. However, when it comes to your brain, alcohol, like cortisol, has a very dark side.

The metabolic breakdown of alcohol in the body leads to the production of a chemical called acetylaldehyde (AH). Aldehyde, as you may know is used to pickle or preserve biological specimens, such as the dead toads we all dissected in high school biology. AH has many negative effects on brain chemistry. It uses up important brain nutrients, especially vitamins B1, B5, and B6. AH also apparently knocks an important enzyme, Acetyl Coenzyme A (CoA) out of circulation. Why is this so bad? Your mitochondria produce almost 90 percent of the ATP (energy) that fuels your body and brain cells. The mitochondria get the raw ingredients (sugar and fat) they need to produce ATP from CoA. CoA is what converts blood sugar into a usable form for ATP production — low CoA, low ATP, low energy. Now you can understand a hangover. Oh yes, alcohol can also increase the free radical load in your brain.

Nutrients Depleted by Alcohol

- DHA
- B Vitamins
- Vitamin C
- Cysteine
- Vitamin E
- Phosphatidyl choline
- Glutamine
- Alpha lipoic acid
- Acetyl-L-Carnitine
- Magnesium

Numerous studies have shown that excessive alcohol consumption, that is, either chronic use (over three drinks a day) or binge drinking (five or more drinks in a short period of time) can significantly impair memory and judgment, attention, and thinking over time. Reaction time on the highway can also be hampered by a few drinks. Excessive alcohol intake shrinks the brain. However, quite remarkably, the brain will start to produce new brain cells about a week after abstinence from chronic alcohol use begins.

I am not saying alcohol is out. But, if you are not a drinker, do not become one. As with most things, moderation is the key. In fact, recent studies have found that red wine in moderation might even be good for your brain. Of course, it is not the alcohol in the wine that is brain beneficial, it is the powerful flavonoids derived from the skin and seeds of the dark grapes. These phenolic compounds are potent neuroprotective antioxidants that can perk up, protect, and preserve your brain cells. But let's not get ahead of ourselves, here. There is still more to learn about about sugar.

Brain AGEing

Perhaps one of the most damaging effects of excess blood sugar is its tendency to react with proteins in the blood to form brain-damaging plaques called advanced glycation end products, or AGEs. Unfortunately, AGEs have a high affinity for sticking to your cerebral capillaries. Excessive high-glycemic carbohydrate consumption and elevated blood sugar can result in accelerated brain AGEing and premature mental decline. In fact, AGEs have been associated with Alzheimer's as well as cardiovascular disease.

The anti-brain glycation effect is simple. AGE plaquelike molecules adhere to the walls of the cerebral capillaries. The capillaries then become inflamed, occluded, and less flexible. In effect, they drastically reduce the flow of vital nutrients to your membranes and mitochondria. What's more, AGEs can also stick to your delicate membranes. This damages the membrane and increases the generation of additional free radicals and inflammation, which further increases free radicals and inflammation within the cell, thus damaging your mighty mitochondria and even DNA.

As a result of this sugar-induced process, over time your thinking can become less flexible and adaptive. Processing speed, mental acuity and agility, and the ability to multitask all decline. Sooner or later, unless dietary levels of high-glycemic carbs are reduced, or certain anti-AGE foods and natural supplements are consumed, neurodegenerative disease sets in.

Now, on that note, we are going to shift gears. Right now you may be feeling that to protect your brain in today's world you are going to have to spend all of your time just dodging brain bullets every which way you turn. Not to worry. Good brain care is really quite simple.

The health and fitness of your brain is controlled by environmental and lifestyle factors more than by your genes. This means that what you breathe, drink and eat (or don't), how much you exercise your body and your brain (or don't), the nutritional supplements you take (or don't), and the amount of stress and anxiety you experience (or don't), all contribute to your brain's performance and efficiency. It also means that you have more control over the fate of your brain than you might think.

When you meet your essential neural needs on a daily basis you can optimize your brain's health and fitness and upgrade its processing power. Almost immediately you experience greater mental productivity, clarity, awareness, and concentration. Best of all, you provide your brain with everything it needs for a long and strong memory. In the next chapter I am going to introduce you to the basics of Neural Need Number One — neural stimulation.

6

Use It Or Lose It

"Another objection to age is that this weakens the memory.
Certainly if you fail to give it exercise..."

Cicero, Cato the Elder on Age, (44 B.C.)

In the sixties, President John F. Kennedy changed our perceptions of exercise when he said "Physical fitness is not only one of the most important keys to a healthy body, it is the basis of dynamic and creative, intellectual activity." This simple shift in our consciousness spawned decades of intense focus on the body — everything from Thigh Masters™ to Nautilus™ machines – barbells, Health Riders™, aerobics, jazzercise, long-distance running, sprinting, spinning, and stepping. For over 30 years we have been obsessed with the look and fitness of our bodies. We have worried fervently about what to eat, and when to eat it, what to do, and when to do it. And thank goodness we have, because there is no longer any doubt that exercise can help protect you from many of the diseases commonly associated with aging, including hypertension, diabetes, cardiovascular disease, osteoporosis, and perhaps even Alzheimer's.

In the 1990s, then President George Bush shifted our focus from the body to the brain. He declared the nineties the decade of the brain. It spawned a tidal wave of scientific research about the brain and the discoveries are still coming forth. We have learned more about the brain and the mind in the past 10 to 15 years than ever before in history.

Science has long debated whether or not injured, damaged, dysfunctional, or dying brain cells can be coaxed or nurtured to stage a comeback. We now know that almost any brain, even adult and senior brains, can be stimulated to grow new neurons, or at least new synapses and connections in certain areas of the brain such as the learning and memory center.

Perhaps tens of thousands of new, baby neurons are born every day in the center of your brain, where your hippocampus resides. The sprouting of these new neurons is called neurogenesis. However, we also now know that the survival of these neophyte neurons is highly tenuous. Stress, environmental toxins, depression, excess alcohol, and a bad brain diet can all lead to their premature death. The good news is that researchers now believe that mental stimulation, curiosity, and learning can help these newly formed neurons to survive, especially if you minimize your exposure to the stress factors that lead to their early demise. Stimulating your neurons with brain speed exercises promotes and protects the health, fitness, and longevity of your brain.

Brain Power

If you want to build muscle power you challenge your muscles with a workout. If you want to build brainpower, what do you do? You challenge your brain with brain-stimulating exercise.

Right about now, you are probably thinking, "Wait a minute, my mind gets all the stimulation it needs. I'm thinking hard all day, every day." In fact, you might even be thinking that your brain is already overstimulated. You are right, on the overstimulated point. Let me assure you, typical thinking is not the kind of mental stimulation I am talking about. It does not help you build brainpower. In fact, it often stresses your brain out.

Neural stimulation is a specific type of brain exercise, not to be confused with ordinary thinking, problem solving, or brainteasers. Neuro-stimulation challenges your brain to fire its synapses faster and faster, which in turn can help your brain develop new brain cells, synapses, and neural connections, which in turn upgrades your brain's processing speed and efficiency. The more new synapses and connections you have, the longer you will hold on to your intelligence, memory, focus, and ability to solve problems and make decisions. Let's take a closer look at how it works.

You and Your IQs

Intelligence is one of the most controversial, misrepresented, and misunderstood concepts in the world. Some years ago, when the book The Bell Curve came out, it spawned a raging nature versus nurture controversy that played out on the front page of national newspapers, on television news, on national talk shows, and in the hallowed halls of academia. The basic premise of the book stated that intelligence was in fact inherited. One camp of cognitive scientists and educational psychologists argued strongly that, yes, intelligence is almost all genetic — you have to play with the hand you have been dealt. Another camp argued that intelligence is only partially a genetic, hereditary factor — that, in fact, it is environmentally shaped and perhaps consciously modifiable. And science has been delving into the matter, no pun intended, ever since. Let's take a moment and examine what we know today about intelligence, or IQ.

The most common measure of intelligence (an IQ test) assesses static or crystallized intelligence – your accumulated knowledge and skills. This is what you know (have learned) including facts, as well as methods of using that information through reasoning, logic, and problem solving. Another equally valid, yet lesser-known, type of intelligence test measures fluid intelligence — how well your brain adapts to change and challenge, or mental flexibility. Officially it has been called on-the-spot reasoning, which is not dependent on your knowledge base. Whereas crystallized intelligence does not appear to decline with age, fluid intelligence, which is based on the health and fitness of your nervous system, does decline significantly with age. These two intelligences are not the same, and yet they are statistically correlated.

Your IQ, as designated by your score on a standard IQ test may be significantly dependent on your fluid intelligence on the day of the test. In turn, your fluid intelligence may be highly dependent upon the speed and efficiency of your cognitive processing that day. Both working (short-term) memory capacity and working memory speed have been highly correlated to IQ scores. Your general or global intelligence, then, is heavily based on the speed of your working memory, or attention and thinking brain, and its communication with your other brains (sensory-motor, learning-memory, and feeling and emoting).

What all of this tells us is that your score on an IQ test is based on your accumulated base of knowledge and how quickly you can remember, reason, and apply it during the test. How much you have learned and how well you can apply it on test day is determined by how fast and efficiently your brain processes (learns, remembers, and applies) information. Does that mean your IQ score can vary? Yes, it does.

Your IQ score can vary significantly, depending on your state of mind during the test. If you were deathly ill, or severely depressed, on the day of your first IQ test it could drastically affect your score. The level of distraction you were experiencing during the test could also play a role in the outcome; for example, taking the test during the emotional stress of the holidays could send your score into the dumpster. Naturally, the reverse is true as well. You could also show up for an IQ test on one of those days when you are completely focused, clear-headed, and sharp, and ace it.

Your IQ can also vary significantly depending on the health and fitness of your brain. For example, your test score could be negatively impacted if you were drunk, or had a head-pounding hangover on the day of test. Even a hypoglycemic blood sugar crash during the test could affect your score. A study of low-IQ inner-city children showed that when they were given high doses of certain B vitamins it increased their IQ test scores by 10 percent or more. Today we know that pregnant and lactating mothers who take vitamins, such as folic acid and choline (derived from soy lecithin) produce babies whose brainpower and mental health are higher than those babies whose moms' diets were low in these factors.

We also know now that in early childhood, and even much later in adult life, being curious, learning, or simply being in an enriched or stimulating environment nourishes the neurons, encourages the sprouting of new neural connections, and significantly sharpens the brain for many years to come.

So what is it that actually makes us smart? Is it the number of brain cells we have, or is it our thoughts and how fast and easily we think them? The answer is brain speed. However, the number of brain cells, synapses, and neural connections (dendrites and axons) contributes mightily to how long we can sustain mental acuity, speed, and memory as we age. It is what we call our cognitive reserve, which could be likened to redundant circuits in a computer. If one circuit goes down there are other circuits that can kick in and take over without missing a beat. If your brain is clobbered by a stroke or head injury it is your cognitive reserves that kick in and try to pick up the slack. Speed, nerve conduction velocity, brain size, amount of grey matter, glucose metabolism and blow flow, and intracranial levels of choline have all been scientifically associated with intelligence.

ECPs...The Muscles of Your Mind

Philosophers over the ages have argued about the nature of thought. Plato believed that thinking resulted from a dialogue between two voices in the mind. He said that thinking was "the talking of the soul with itself". Einstein and many other creative geniuses have alluded to pure thought as an intuitive process that often runs counter to logic. And, in fact, many great scientific theories and insights have been the result of a sudden flash in the mind of the scientist. Nikola Tesla, the father of the alternating current (AC) generator and motor, invented them while walking in New York City's Central Park one day. In one brilliant moment the formula came to him and he scribbled it in the dirt with a stick. Was it intuition, or precognition? Maybe you are thinking that means extra sensory perception. It does not. Precognition refers to the information processing stages that precede cognition, that is, the formation of a thought. Tesla's brain was most likely processing various elements of the formula before they all came together and crystallized into a complete thought.

Cognitive scientists tell us that the very process of thinking is made up of discrete stages of information processing. They are called elementary cognitive processes, or ECPs. Here is a list of the various ECPs that make up our thoughts.

- Registration: perception of external or internal stimuli — the view of an orchard while you are driving through the country
- Categorization: placing the registered stimuli into a category — it is an apple tree orchard
- Identification: identifying the stimuli and unconsciously deciding

whether it is relevant (meaningful) for further processing — they are Red Delicious apples and I think I want to stop and pick some of these apples

- Organization: encoding and consolidating the information for immediate consideration or storage — I think I may want to come back to this orchard next fall
- Storage: filing the encoded information for future retrieval and use — so I will remember where I want to come back to
- Retrieval: recalling the pertinent information — remembering how to get to the orchard a year later
- Executive: processing perceived or retrieved information to solve a problem, make a decision, conduct planning, or take action — deciding to drive back to the orchard

It has been hypothesized that it takes over a second to form a simple, basic thought, and that each thought is actually made up of a series of several of these sequential subcomponents, or ECPs. For example, if you are out walking in the park and a man approaches with a big growling dog that is straining at its leash and moving rapidly in your direction, you register and categorize dog, recognize teeth, retrieve and compare information that correlates this experience with danger, feel fear, and decide to move out of the way. And, all of this happens in less than a second.

Such automatic thinking is based on a matrix of hundreds, if not thousands, of associations between past experiences, thoughts, and associated emotions. When ECPs function quickly and efficiently problem solving, decision making, multitasking, planning, and organizing all work better. ECPs are like the little muscles of your brain. When they are fit, healthy, and cocoordinated, and all working together, the result is optimal mental performance.

It is now becoming more widely recognized that the first signs of accelerated, premature cognitive decline occur when one or more of these ECPs slows down. For instance, before actual memory capacity declines, that is, how much you can remember, the speed of recalling recently learned material declines. Normally, as we age, we all experience a slowing in our ability to provide a smart answer to an unexpected question, or to recall names, places, and important facts that we know we know. The greater the pressure to immediately perform (a demand on speed), or the more difficult, challenging, or complex the decision or problem, the more dramatically our speed and efficiency drop off. The higher the cognitive load in any situation we face, the more we are slowed down by our age. This may be due to a weakening in those little muscles of our mind — the ECPs.

A 100-meter sprinter can train exclusively by running wind sprints. However, if weight training is added to her daily running regimen her running muscles will also gain strength. This will not only give her explosive power coming out of the blocks, it will also give her the speed and endurance she needs to cross the finish line a winner. The key to smarter thinking, a better memory, and greater mental productivity may lie in exercising your ECPs — strengthening each of your mental muscles — thus stimulating your brain cells to grow and sprout new cerebral connections for faster communication.

Cognition Ignition — ECTs for Your ECPs

Brain building is best accomplished by exercising your ECPs with elementary cognitive tasks, or ECTs. Typically these ECTs involve the use of highly stimulating brain speed tests, exercises, and even games that challenge our ability to stay focused, be quick, and remember. ECTs challenge your brain to process information more quickly, more efficiently, and more precisely. Each ECT stimulates a specific part of your brain. By responding to each task as rapidly as you can you stimulate and invigorate that particular region of the brain.

Let's take a closer look at the specific cognitive processes of your brains, and what you can do to boost their performance. Each of your brains — sensory and motor, learning and memory, attention and thinking, and feeling and emoting — has its own subdivisions and processing centers. And, they are interconnected, much like your "knee bone's connected to your thigh bone".

Your S&M brain handles sensory (visual, auditory, and sensual) stimuli input, or stimulation. It has a speed of processing incoming information and a speed of reacting (motor response), when appropriate. For example, you see a dog run in front of your car, you hit the brakes. Your physical reaction time is also known as your motor reflexes.

Your speed of seeing is something different. It is how fast you see. In effect it is what you actually see before you are conscious (or acknowledge) that you are seeing it or how much you see in a given moment. Hitting a 99 mph fast ball requires superior seeing and reacting, visual and motor, speed.

Quickly spotting a child lost in a large group of people requires superior speed of scanning and pattern recognition (identification). This is defined by how fast the neurons in your sensory brain and pathways can process information. As with other types of brain performance, seeing speed is improvable with visual processing speed exercises. In fact, you can easily train your brain to see what may actually be subliminal for most other people. Seeing speed also determines how alert you are.

Your S&M brain processes raw incoming data, unconsciously organizes it, and then refers what is relevant to your A&T brain to act on or file away. Its effectiveness is based on how quickly and efficiently each task is performed. Focused attention, memory (learning and recall), decision making, multitasking, and mental flexibility and agility are all improvable with neuro-stimulating brain exercises that challenge your mind, senses, and body to see, learn, recall, and respond as quickly as possible.

Your L&M brain acts as a switchboard for the routing, consolidation, storage, and retrieval of memories. It stores memories coming in from your A&T brain, and it also retrieves short-term memories that your A&T brain directs it to look for. The speed and efficiency of information exchange between your A&T and L&M brains determine how well memories are formed, stored, and recalled.

Your F&E brain also plays a role in your ECPs and mental performance. The strongest memories are those that were stored with the extra energy of emotion such as fear, anxiety, excitement, or ecstasy. Emotion can also be a powerful factor in how well you perform. Poor performance on an IQ test or exam, for instance, can be the result of fear, anxiety, even depression, and not necessarily inferior intelligence or a faulty memory.

Properly designed ECT speed exercises enable you to isolate and exercise each of the ECPs: perception, categorization and identification, consolidation and storage, retrieval and executive application of information for decision making, planning, problem solving, reasoning, and taking action. Practicing ECTs for your ECPs improves your overall focus, thinking, and mental performance, just as exercising specific muscle groups can enhance athletic performance.

A high-performance, speedy brain can strategically position you ahead of the pack. It means finishing tasks faster so you have more time and energy for the finer things in life – your family, friends, and community. The quicker your brain, the smarter your thinking, the more you get done. Faster brains can handle more of the information overload we are exposed to day in and day out. The more you can handle, the less bogged down your brain will feel. And, a fit and healthy, high-performance brain means a fit and healthy high-performance mind and body for life.

When you challenge a muscle with exercise it gets stronger and more powerful. When you challenge your brain to work faster you build new brain cells and connections and that equals more brainpower. A British study showed that London cabbies had more grey matter in the area of the brain used to remember navigation details such as their position on a map, their destination, and the direction they need to travel to get there and back. This is called visual-spatial orientation and memory. Apparently the taxi drivers in the study actually grew bigger brains through the neuro-stimulating practice of frequently learning new routes. Active curiosity and learning, especially speed learning, can build a bigger, better, faster brain.

Mentathletes

A decathlete just may be the ultimate athlete, participating in the 10 events of a decathlon, each challenging the strength, power, and endurance of a different set of muscles. Decathletes must exercise all of the muscles in each section of the body to achieve the explosive speed and endurance necessary for each event. Training increases the athlete's performance quotient exponentially.

A mentathlete then might be someone who excels in all the powers of mind – he or she is quick to learn, remember, reason, and react. However, there is a big difference in the way a decathlete and a mentathlete need to train. Becoming a mentathlete is within the grasp of virtually anyone committed to meeting his or her brain's three vital daily needs – neuro-stimulation, neuro-nutrition, and neuro-napping.

The faster your brain's processing speed, the more focused you are, the more you take in and learn, the more you remember, the quicker you can make sound, split-second decisions and react. And, this new brainpower not only serves you well in your profession and weekend athletic challenges, it will make you sharper, smarter, and more alert in all areas of your life.

A senior high school physics teacher asked his students whom they perceived as the brightest and most capable in the class. Was it the best athletes, or the best gamers, or the students with the highest grades? No, those perceived as smartest were those who appeared swiftest on their feet, quickest with their wit, and fastest on the draw – the mentathletes. It is so true; down through the ages we have referred to a person we view as smart and successful as quick, sharp as a tack, or fast on his or her feet. Conversely, someone considered less intelligent is often referred to as slow.

Exercising your ECPs with fun and easy ECTs can stimulate your brain to sprout new synapses and grow new connections. It is the key to smarter thinking, a better memory, and greater mental productivity, for life.

Learning a new process or language, mastering a new computer game or program, learning to play a musical instrument or do a new dance routine, pursuing a new career or developing a new hobby or skill such as knitting, can all stimulate your brain to nurture new neural connections and brain cells, at any age. Bear in mind, once a process or skill is learned the neurotrophic effects seem to wear off. Brain cells can be fickle — once the challenge is gone, growth (and brainpower) can plateau, if not shrivel and decline. So, you have got to keep stimulating your brain. It just won't let you rest on your laurels.

Old Brains, New Tricks

PET scan and MRI images of the brain show that every time you engage your brain in a stimulating activity, or challenge it with a neuro-cognitive task, certain brain areas light up brilliantly. The challenge can be as simple as having a series of license plates flashed in front of you one after another, and then testing how quickly you can recall the numbers and letters. On a PET scan the activated or challenged processing centers of your brain light up in brilliant red, yellow, and orange colors during a memory challenge like this. This indicates a sharp rise in glucose metabolism and increased blood flow to that part of the brain being challenged. What's more, it shows that specifically designed mental challenges can warm up and develop any part of the brain or brain processing center that you want to target. It is similar to the way a Nautilus machine works by isolating specific muscle groups.

Stimulated neural activity, such as brain speed exercise, not only increases blood flow and brain cell uptake of glucose and oxygen, it also places a significantly higher demand on the delivery of other vital nutrients, such as brain-specific amino acids that fuel the manufacture of your performance-enhancing neurotransmitters. If your diet or nutritional supplements lack these brain-essential aminos, your mental performance may suffer, especially when your brain is under pressure to perform.

Of course, what I am talking about throughout this book is thinking. But, what I am really mean is thinking faster, more efficiently, and smarter – not necessarily thinking harder or longer. Most of our routine thinking is automatic, relatively unconscious and unoriginal, and too often stressful. Most of our daily thinking is a rehash of what we already know, rather than a process of discovery, of learning something new, or reorganizing old information in innovative and productive new ways.

When the fitness revolution was launched in the seventies, the lingering cry of the couch potato was, "Hey, I'm active all day long. Why do I need to exercise any more?" Of course, walking from your house to your car, from the parking lot to your office, from your office to the vending machine does not really qualify as exercise. In the same vein, our daily mental activity is to brain building what mundane daily physical activity is to bodybuilding — it is not the same. And it does not yield the same results.

Most daily mental activity just plain tires the brain out. During a hard day of thinking at work or even at home, the brain often feels foggy by mid-afternoon and fatigued, if not fried, by the end of the day. This is exactly when friends or family want, and need, us to be perky, patient, and present. However, there is a simple remedy. Just like a good workout at the gym or a great run, hike, or brisk walk can leave you feeling up, supercharged, and ready to go, a 10-minute brain tune-up and speed workout can energize your brain and restore your clarity and focus for the rest of the day. In our next chapter you are going to learn all about the art and science of brain speed exercise.

7

Neuro-Stimulation

The Art and Science of Brain Speed Exercise

"If thinking harder and longer were all it took to make us quicker and smarter, we'd all be Einsteins."

Joshua Reynolds

Popular television game shows like "Jeopardy" are based on how fast contestants can dredge the depths of their memory banks, recall the appropriate information, and push a button that signals they know the answer. This game is actually a form of brain speed challenge. The mere act of sitting at home and trying to beat the game-show contestants to the punch line, or at least attempting to answer the question as fast as you can, is also brain speed exercise. It challenges your brain to process information as quickly as it can, thereby revving up your brain cells to fire faster.

Other brain speed challenges, such as completing crossword puzzles or doing math problems as fast a possible, playing a game of speed chess, rapidly scanning a large crowd for a familiar face, or simply typing with as much speed as you can muster are also constructive ways to stimulate your brain. The key to brain speed exercise is not how hard the question or challenge is, but how hard you push for the fastest possible response.

One of my favorite forms of brain speed exercise is what I call speed seeing. This is where you search, or scan for something, as fast as possible. For instance, looking for a certain plate, cup, bowl, or glass in your kitchen cabinet, or a shirt, dress, or pair of slacks or shoes in your clothes closet, or a tool in your tool shed, or a specific item on the shelf at the supermarket. These are all ways to fire up your brain's visual processing neurons. The games often printed on kids' menus at family restaurants or on cereal boxes that require you to search for certain letters, embedded among many other distracting letters or images, can be used as brain speed exercise. This visual-spatial letter (or object) search task, if done as fast as you can, is another way to exercise and increase your brain speed.

Searching for just about anything as fast as you can revs up and integrates the synapses along your sensory-perceptual (S&M) and your attention (A&T) brain pathways. When you do it frequently, as exercise, it will greatly sharpen your senses.

You can also try the brain speed exercise games that I developed over the years. All you have to do is go to www.MyBrainTrainer.com/2020. These exercise games are the best way to improve focus, thinking, memory, and mental quickness. You can do them at home, at work, even on vacation – anywhere you have computer Internet access. They provide a very structured, comprehensive, intense workout and take only a few minutes per day. The more you do them, the more positive the changes, the faster and more long lasting the results. And, if you don't have web access I am going to give you some exercises in this chapter that can help you upgrade your brain speed.

In the same way that a Nautilus machine can be used to isolate and exercise specific muscles or muscle groups (biceps, triceps, or pecs), the following brain speed exercises can stimulate and challenge your various brain muscles – particularly those involved in the functioning of your sensory and motor, attention and thinking, and learning and memory brains.

Sensory-Motor Brain Speed

Your sensory brain processes incoming information. Your motor brain is responsible for your physical reflexes, or reactions. See a red light, step on the brakes. This is your S&M brain in action. Sensory processing speed defines how fast you can register and identify an external stimulus – the red light. Motor speed, or physical reaction time, defines how fast you can react to it – step on the brakes. For example, let's say you are speeding down a country road, round a bend, and there it is…a stop sign. The amount of time it takes your brain to process the information and then send a message to the motor neurons in your leg muscles to slam on the brakes is your physical reaction time. It is the speed at which the information travels from sensory input, or the perception of the stop sign, to a motor reflex, or hitting the brakes.

A physical reaction typically does not demand much cognitive processing because there is little choice involved – you did not have to think about stopping. How quickly you notice the stop sign and react does, of course, require attention (A&T brain). However, after that your brain relegates the responsibility of decision and action or reaction to your sensory and motor brain, sparing you and your higher executive resources from having to think about it. That is pretty smart of your brain since a physical reaction typically takes 250 to 300 milliseconds (ms), far less than the time it would take your conscious mind to think about it, let alone react.

People with very quick reflexes can react to a stimulus such as the unexpected appearance of a stop sign in under 200 ms. Interestingly, the elderly, the intoxicated, the depressed, the cognitively impaired, and those on certain medications, such as sedatives, respond more slowly, with reaction times of well over 400 ms. At sixty miles per hour (eighty-eight feet per second) a 150 millisecond difference in physical reaction time can translate to almost 15 feet, a pretty big margin of error — big enough to mean the difference between life and death.

Physiology textbooks state that the limit of our sensory (perception) motor (reaction) response is 150 ms. And, there are those who believe this pathway is actually hardwired in every individual, thus making it virtually impossible to improve reaction time. However, many thousands of reaction time tests administered over the Internet revealed that with practice most people can significantly improve their reflexes. In my own case I trained my reaction time

Brain Exercise #1
Sensory and Motor Reflex Exercise

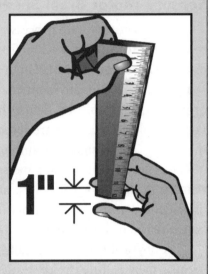

For this exercise you need the assistance of a friend and a 12-inch ruler. Hold your hand out in front of you with your thumb and index finger extended. Your two fingers should have approximately one inch of space between them. Have your friend hold a foot-long ruler vertically above your hand. The ruler should be positioned so that the one-inch mark is at the top and the 12-inch mark is at the bottom, closest to your hand.

Direct your friend to unexpectedly release the ruler so it passes between your two fingers. Your objective is to catch the ruler before it escapes your grasp and hits the ground. You are not to move your hand or fingers up or down in an attempt to catch it. You must keep them steady, in the same place, and at the same height from the floor. You simply want to grasp the ruler as it passes between your thumb and index finger.

Do this 10 times in succession. Each time you catch the ruler write down the inch mark where your fingers have grasped it. This is a way for you to record your progress, to see how many inches the ruler fell before you could catch it, and to see how much more quickly you are able to catch it with practice. Initially, you may not be able to catch the ruler at all. However, with practice you will train your sensory and motor brain to react more rapidly. Practicing this technique can help develop your reflexes.

from 220 milliseconds down to 160 ms, something once believed virtually impossible for anyone, let alone a 60-something senior. Brain Exercise #1 is a fun exercise you can use to train your physical, motor reflexes right in your own kitchen or living room.

Seeing Speed

Imagine standing at home plate, facing a Roger Clemens fastball. Most of us would be lucky even to see the ball, much less hit it. Another brain muscle or ECP in your sensory and motor brain is the processing of perceptual stimuli. This defines how fast you can see, or how much you can visually process per millisecond. Perceptual processing speed determines whether or not you can see a 98 mph fastball before it goes flying by you. Faster seeing allows you to see a fastball as if it were traveling at a much slower speed.

When you are driving, faster seeing allows you to notice someone pulling out of an obscure side road and into your lane before the car is right in front of you. Large group studies involving the elderly have shown that speed training programs significantly improve driving skills and safety records.

Interestingly, pharmaceutical companies often determine how a drug is affecting a person's brain by testing his or her seeing speed. In this kind of test, subjects are asked to report when the gradually increasing flashing, or flicker rate, of a strobe light finally appears to them as a steady or solid light — when it no longer appears to be flickering. The number of flickers per second at which your brain can no longer discriminate a flashing light is defined as your critical flicker fusion frequency. Typically, the average person's perceptual threshold of discrimination is around 25 to 30 cycles per second. Normally, if someone is intoxicated, hungover, sleepless, or depressed their flicker fusion frequency is lower, because they see more slowly. In other words, the neurons in their visual processing circuits are working less efficiently, or are less sensitive to their normal threshold level of perception. Again, this reflects what I call seeing speed.

Challenging your visual processes can improve your perceptual acuity, or seeing speed. Put another way, if you have heightened perceptual acuity, or seeing speed, you can actually see more per unit of time than others. In relation to the baseball player, the faster he can see — the slower and bigger the ball seems to be. Great ballplayers often comment that when they are in the zone the ball looks fat, as well as slow. This lets them perceive it earlier in its path to home plate, and determine sooner whether it is a curve, sinker, slider, and in the strike zone. Of course, add this perceptual acuity to greater physical reflexes and they have a considerable advantage over the pitcher, even if it is Roger Clemens or Randy Johnson.

Even if you are not a ballplayer, a racquetball or squash player, or a weekend warrior on the tennis court or football field, exercising your speed of visual processing will allow you to see things sooner so you have more time to adjust to the unexpected. For instance, recent research has shown that seeing speed correlates highly with driver safety records, especially with the number of injury accidents. Researchers have trained slow drivers to see and react faster. The net result was significantly improved driving safety records as evidenced by a reduced number of injury accidents

So, how does improved seeing speed affect your daily routine? Well, if the cat springs across the kitchen counter dive-bombing a shadow, causing your favorite crystal vase to fall towards the floor, you will have a much better chance of rescuing the vase before it hits the ground. Or, suppose you are in a public place and something or someone moving very fast comes into the periphery of your vision. It could be a ball, a stone, a falling object, maybe even a purse-snatcher, but whatever it is it is coming like a bat out of hell. Quite fortunately you sense it in a split second — soon enough to take action. However, if your visual acuity, or seeing speed, is even slightly off, chances are you are going to get clobbered.

Brain Exercise #2
Perceptual Acuity and Seeing Speed Exercise

Although perceptual acuity is part of your sensory and motor brain, it is different from your physical reaction time. It is how fast you can see, or detect something right as it is happening. Just about anyone can quickly develop his or her speed seeing ability with brain speed training.

Here is a great, and safe, seeing speed exercise you can do when you are driving. Scan the road in front of you, then on either side, as quickly as possible – without moving your head. When you approach an intersection, or want to change lanes on the highway, scan what is in front of you and to either side as fast as you can. Rapid scanning allows you to actually see more, and eventually see faster. Rapid scanning is a safer way to drive, because you will tend to see more, such as accidents "about to happen". That means you can avoid them. Plus, speed scanning stimulates your brain cells to work quicker. You will be amazed at how much faster your reflexes are when you react to something unexpected, like catching an open container that falls out of the refrigerator when you open the door, or avoiding someone who darts into the street in front of your car. When someone tosses a set of keys at you and shouts "think fast," you will, and you will surprise anyone who sees you in action.

A good athlete, even an average sportsman, or an adversary or challenger in your field of work can get the best of you by catching you off guard. How sensitive or alert your sensory brain cells are can often spell the difference between whether you rise to the challenge or not. Winning or losing on the athletic field or court, success or failure in the professional arena, and life or death on the highway can all be impacted by seeing speed. The good news is you can train your brain to be more alert, and your eyes to see more with some simple speed seeing exercises.

Attention and Thinking Speed

Let's stay at home plate for a moment longer. Once you have tuned up your physical and perceptual reflexes and acuity you have a better chance of actually hitting the ball. That is, unless the pitcher mixes it up a bit and throws you curves, then fastballs, then sliders, then a few sinkers, and then goes back to a steady barrage of fastballs. In this situation you have a choice to make, quickly. Once your sharpened perceptual processor picks the ball up closer to its release point, and you can determine the type of pitch it is, you then have a few hundred milliseconds to choose the type of swing you are going to take. Or not take, if your split-second calculations tell your arm muscle's motor neurons that the ball is going to be out of the strike zone. Now remember, this whole process of seeing, adjusting, deciding and reacting to the ball takes about 400 ms, far less time than it takes to form a thought. In fact, you don't want to think about it, or you will strike out. Another brilliant example of how wonderful a computing machine your brain really is.

Speed thinking stimulates the executive headquarters of your brain to work faster, to be more focused, and efficient. In essence, you can process more decision or problem solving cycles per second. This improves your mental productivity. Survival, winning, looking sharp in any fast-moving challenge requires this kind of mental quickness — on the highway, in an athletic competition, in a sales meeting or skull session, or in a classroom debate, speedier thinking gives you the edge.

Suppose you are watching "Jeopardy" and you want to impress your children, or grandchildren, with how quick you are. You can, with even slightly upgraded thinking speed. After a little speed thinking exercise, in that next game of bridge, poker, backgammon, or chess you play you will make sound, split-second decisions that will amaze your opponents, and put you in the winner's circle.

Venus Williams, the tennis champ, has a serve that has been clocked at 125 mph. That's fast. At that speed the ball is moving at 176 feet per second. Since the length of tennis court is 120 feet, her opponent has a little over a half-second to react to the ball. This means she first has to see the ball coming off the head of Venus's racquet, then figure out its direction, where it might land, whether it is slicing or hooking, how much topspin it has, and so on. Typically this multiple choice calculation and decision would take seconds to process. Then the opponent has to react, moving her body and racket into position, swinging, and hitting the ball back. This complex process requires sensory and motor, attention and thinking, and learning and memory pathways all to be integrated into one fast, harmonious system — impossible for most people, even at Wimbledon. That is, unless you have speed trained your brain to boost your seeing, decision-making, and reaction times.

Attention and Thinking Speed Exercises

Your attention and thinking brain (the executive headquarters) handles incoming data ranging from automatic registration, such as the scenery on a car ride to a question someone asks you (or you ask yourself), to information you are trying to learn such as a new computer program, game, language, even dance step. For example, if someone asks you what 16 times 24 equals, the speed with which you perform the computation is a function of your A&T brain's processing power. Your A&T, or executive, brain speed (what psychologists call working memory) has been scientifically correlated with IQ, logic and reasoning powers, attention, and learning. You already know from Chapter 5 that many factors can affect this power. Intoxication or a hangover, a cold or a headache, even a thick head can significantly slow down and dull your A&T brain.

Brain Exercise #3 should be done once a day for a minimum of three minutes. Three minutes on most challenging brain speed exercises is enough neuro-stimulation time to increase the blood flow, oxygen, glucose, and other nutrients to your brain. The number of completed (but not necessarily correct) problems processed becomes your score. Your objective is to complete more and more computations during each three-minute exercise session you perform.

If you can process all 40 math problems in three minutes – GREAT! Increase the number of problems to 60 and try to do those in three minutes. Mental calculation speed has been correlated to intelligence, reasoning ability, and problem solving. Why? Because the more information you can process in a given period of

Brain Exercise #3
Attention and Thinking Speed Exercise

Here is an example of an attention and thinking exercise that can sharpen your brain speed and executive powers.

Write down a list of 40 simple math problems, or use the ones below. Use an equal number (such as 10) of multiplication, division, addition and subtraction problems. Use computations such as:

Multiplication	Division	Addition	Subtraction
19×6	$54 \div 9$	$38 + 74$	$66 - 28$
42×3	$66 \div 33$	$65 + 83$	$77 - 44$
54×5	$84 \div 4$	$93 + 66$	$93 - 52$
72×6	$96 \div 6$	$33 + 41$	$83 - 59$
83×7	$42 \div 6$	$52 + 51$	$33 - 26$
27×4	$64 \div 4$	$16 + 27$	$13 - 9$
36×2	$15 \div 5$	$57 + 42$	$88 - 14$
91×9	$22 \div 11$	$27 + 37$	$22 - 8$
41×3	$44 \div 10$	$63 + 22$	$39 - 19$
21×2	$32 \div 2$	$12 + 11$	$63 - 39$

Take a few minutes to process these calculations as fast as you can. Try to do as much of the calculating in your head as possible. Write down each answer and quickly speed on to the next problem.

Don't worry about making mistakes. Accuracy is important but *in brain speed training it is most important to push your synapses to fire faster*. It is the utter determination to be focused and quick that best stimulates your brain to stretch, grow, and regenerate.

time, the more decision cycles, or problem solving alternatives you can entertain, and effectively execute.

Another attention and thinking speed exercise you can do is really a fun game, but its effect on your brain is the same as an exercise. It is called "Pig" and it was a tradition in my family when I was growing up. Just recently, at a family reunion I played it again, with cousins, nephews, and nieces and enjoyed it more then ever. You can play it with two or more people, but the more the better.

Brain Exercise #4
Pig – A reflex game

You start with the following props: enough plastic or wooden clothespins for each player, a set of dice, a pot lid, and some strong string. Tie each clothespin tightly with the string, and then cut it about two feet from the clothespin. Each pig now has a two-foot tail.

The play starts with a selected player rolling the dice while he or she holds the pot lid on the floor in front of him. Each of the other players, sitting in a cricle places their pig, that is the clothespin, in the center of the circle, and hangs on to the end of the string, ready to pull it out of the circle as fast as possible if the roller tosses a 7 or 11. The roller's challenge is to lift the lid and slam it down on top of as many slow-reacting pigs as he or she can whenever a 7 or 11 comes up. The roller can also fake out the other players by lifting the lid and pretending he or she is going to trap you when he rolls something other than a 7 or 11. If you yank your pig out when the roll isn't a 7 or 11, you lose.

Scoring is as follows (we used to play for a nickel a point):

1. Roller gets a point for each pig trapped

2. Roller gets a point for each pig that gets prematurely yanked (by a trigger-happy player jumping the gun) during a fake strike on a non-7 or 11 roll.

3. Players each get a point if the roller gets trigger-happy and slams down the lid when neither a 7 or 11 is rolled.

4. Players get a point if they get their pig out before the roller traps them on a 7 or 11 roll.

5. Players get a point if the roller lifts the pot lid before the dice come to a rest.

The roller loses his or her turn to the player on the right either when all the players escape on a 7 or 11 roll, or the roller mistakenly slams the pot lid down on all pigs remaining in the center when neither a 7 or 11 was rolled. The roller also loses one point for each pig that he or she erroneously traps.

This is a brain speed challenge for both the player and roller and it promises to get the adrenaline pumping and the laughter roaring.

Mental Flexibility and Agility

Mental flexibility is the ability to react to the unknown, to quickly adjust to a sudden and unexpected situation. For example, let's pretend it's Super Bowl Sunday and you are one of the starting quarterbacks. The opposing defense has been blitzing you on every play. So you have been releasing the ball as quickly as possible on each play. All of a sudden, on the next play, when you are expecting a blitz it doesn't come. Your brain quickly adjusts and reacts appropriately. You hit your wide receiver sprinting down the sideline and it is a touchdown.

Athletes, business executives, operating room surgeons, nurses, bus drivers, trial attorneys, police officers, and soldiers in battle often have to react quickly and confidently in tense moments when they are faced with something unexpected. The speed of their adjustment to rapid and unexpected change often spells the difference between success and failure, even life or death. Mental flexibility, like physical flexibility, is improvable with the right types of cognitive exercise. Speed exercise is like Yoga for the brain.

Mental agility is your brain's ability to simultaneously process, calculate or compute a significant number of options, that is, multitask, then make the appropriate decision and take the right action. The chess player who has to review his opponent's board and compute the next five or six possible permutations of moves, the business executive who must articulate his or her company's financial status to the Board of Directors, the salesman who has to respond quickly when a potential buyer is firing questions at him left and right, and the mother who has three kids all requiring her attention at the same time, all need mental agility to cope, if not to win or succeed.

Look around you. What happens to most people as they get older? They not only slow down, they lose their flexibility and agility. Often, thinking and reacting become highly structured, rigid, and inflexible. Challenging your brain's ability to handle more information simultaneously, faster, and more efficiently builds your mental agility and flexibility. What's more, a spontaneous, flexible, and agile mind leads to a healthier, potentially longer living brain.

Mental flexibility and agility training is fun and phenomenally helpful in gaining that decided mental advantage in virtually anything you do. What's more, mental agility is attractive. People admire the quick witted, those able to handle themselves well when confronted with a seemingly overwhelming number of options that they must quickly process and respond to.

Let's recap for a moment. Your A&T, or executive, processor is involved in just about all of your reflexes, at least when attention is necessary. Of course the brain also registers stimuli unconsciously, which does not involve A&T processing – until or unless a decision or other mental response is called for.

Much of what we call thinking is automatic, and takes place in less than a second. For example, reacting to a tennis ball coming over the net does not really require you to think. However, mental flexibility and agility, as I have defined it, deals with integrated sensory-executive-physical reaction performance that is faster than thinking. That means you know you have to hit the ball back across the net, but don't have to stop and take the time to think about how hard to hit it and where to place it so you can win the game.

Next, we are going to discuss thinking speed. After all, we do think and thinking is made up of many ECPs. If these subcomponents of thought are working faster and more efficiently, then the result will be faster thinking.

Thinking Speed

The thinking, or executive, process takes place in your A&T brain, also known as your prefrontal cortex. It is here that your so-called working memory is located. Remember, you have two types of memory – short-term, working memory, or RAM, and long-term memory. Working memory is like a sketch pad for words, thoughts, names, facts and visual images that are briefly held conscious by your A&T brain while it is engaged in planning, decision making, problem solving and reasoning.

Imagine you are in a Poker Challenge in Las Vegas. There are eight people at your table. It is Seven-Card Stud. The stakes are high and your mind is feeling a little fuzzy. You look around and begin to feel like you might be in over your head.

You get dealt three cards, two down and one up. You look around at the seven other hands. The betting starts. You can drop or stay in. Next round, everyone gets another card up. Your executive processor continues calculating – what kind of hands your opponents might be building, what cards they think you have, are they betting like they have a strong hand, or are they bluffing. Are they falling for your bluff? Each round your working memory has more information and options to remember, consider, calculate, and decide. Your decision gets tougher…stay or drop. Fear triggers old emotions about losing (F&E brain). The old inappropriate emotions cloud your mind. Your executive processor starts bogging down. This is a sure formula for losing. You wish you had done more brain speed exercises before plunking down that $500 to enter the Tournament.

Working memory has two qualities, speed and capacity. Both are related. The faster you can mentally recite, or rehearse, a long list of items on a shopping list the more likely it is that you will come home with everything on the list. Speed allows your working memory, RAM processor to temporarily hold more information. Working memory also has a short-term memory capacity somewhat independent of speed. For instance, a test that is commonly given in psychology experiments is the reverse digit span test. This is where a number of letters or digits is shown to

Brain Exercise #5
Thinking Speed and Memory

Here is a combined working memory speed and paired-association memory challenge. Paired-association memory is what you use when you can put a name to a face; the two are associated in your memory banks.

Take a full deck of cards and pull out all the face cards (the four Jacks, Queens, Kings and Aces). Take half of these 16 cards, arrange them in a vertical column, face-up. Now randomly draw a card from the rest of the deck and place one beside each of the face cards, also face-up.

Now you have a column of cards with the faces showing and right beside each is a corresponding number card, face-up. Take one minute to memorize each associated pair, the face card and its associated number card. Write them down on a piece of paper.

Now, turn the 16 cards over and mix them together.

Write down the exact time and then begin:

Turn over (face-up) all 16 cards and see how many you can pair them up in three minutes. Note: you do not have to put them in the same order, just correct associated pairing. Do as many as you can as quickly as possible without slowing down to think about it. Don't worry if you have a few unpaired cards. Don't labor over them; this is a speed test. Don't guess either, just pair up the ones you actually remember. When the three minutes are up, write down the number you correctly paired up. That's your score.

you, and then you have to repeat them in exact reverse order. This is a test of short-term, working memory capacity. Obviously, you are not expected to remember the letters a few days or even hours later. It is very short-term memory only.

The average person's A&T brain starts bogging down around seven items – words, letters, objects or whatever. The number of letters you can recall in reverse order is closely correlated to your IQ. Now here is the interesting part. With training, many people can dramatically improve their working memory capacity to dozens of items. Some researchers claim that this simple exercise can help just about anyone stretch their short-term memory capacity, and perhaps intelligence.

Other Great A&T Exercises

- Speed chess
- Speed crossword puzzles
- Many card games including poker, bridge, and hearts where quick thinking and/or memory is involved
- Learning a new computer program, playing reaction time thinking games, even Tetris.

Remember This

Developing a superior memory is not only possible it is probable, if you do the right exercises with the right muscles of your mind. You can increase your memory power so that you can more easily remember names, phone numbers, addresses, PIN numbers or items on a shopping list? You have just learned how to challenge, train, and improve your short-term memory capacity, which is what you use to remember details like names and numbers that you are going to use in the next few moments. You can also train your brain to better encode new information so you can form stronger, more long-lasting memories. How well your mind focuses your A&T brain on the information at hand and how well it rehearses that information in the ensuing minutes after you focus on it, determines how well the information gets encoded, consolidated, and filed away for successful long-term memory storage and subsequent retrieval.

Long-term memory, such as remembering a phone number the day after you learn it, not only depends on how well your A&T brain's focus engraved the information into your short-term memory sketch pad, it is also dependent on a number of other variables: how important the information is to you, whether there is a strong emotion associated with the memory, and even how well you sleep that night.

Research studies have shown that exercises that challenge your working memory (your attention and thinking brain) also stimulate your learning and memory center, especially if your intention is to remember the information. This results in increased blood flow and activated metabolism in the memory center and pathways in your brain, as well as an increase in the uptake of neurotransmitters specific to learning and memory. The learning process can even trigger the brain's production of nerve growth factors, which stimulates the birth of new neural connections (neurites, or axons and dendrites) and possibly synapses.

Remember, it has only recently been discovered that the learning and memory center of the brain gives birth to new neurons every day. Unfortunately, these baby brain cells tend to die off unless their environment is nourishing and nurturing. Quite remarkably, it is now believed that the very process of learning something new not only keeps these baby neurons alive, it stimulates them to rapidly develop into mature, fully functional neurons within a matter of weeks. Perhaps this is why Alzheimer's disease and later-life memory decline are inversely related to both the number of years of formal education and the level of intellectual activity, such as crossword puzzles, bridge, chess, and other games and hobbies in your midlife years.

When you look up a telephone number or get it from the operator and then hold it actively in your mind as you go to dial it, you are using your A&T brain's short-term working memory. If you don't use the number right away, and you stop rehearsing it, and then have to remember it a few minutes, hours, or days later you are using your learning and memory brain's longer term, delayed memory. This is what most people assume is memory, something that gets learned and stored away for later retrieval — everything from childhood school memories to who you saw the movie Titanic with, for example.

When you meet someone new at a cocktail party, hear his or her name, then address him or her later you may find that you have forgotten the person's name in just a few minutes. Of course, there are several factors that can contribute to this. One is the attention you give the person when he or she is introduced. Another is the conscious rehearsal of his or her name. Yet another is the number of distractions and cocktails at the party that contribute to the rapid fading of these new memory traces.

The good news is that you can improve your memory by focusing your attention on the person as you are being introduced and then rehearsing his or her name with a picture of his or her face in your mind. You can also use recall speed training exercises to sharpen your memory. Brain Exercise #6 was designed to build your memory recall powers.

Brain Exercise #6
Memory Power Exercise

You are going to use a deck of shuffled cards. Turn five cards over, taking about one second per card. Try to memorize each card as you turn it over. After turning over the fifth card, quickly push those five together in a stack and turn them face-down so you can't see the numbers. Now, say out loud as many of the cards as you can remember, as fast as possible. Keep the cards in a stack and move them aside. You do not have to check the stack to see how many you got right. That comes later.

Next do this again with seven new cards, turning over one every second, trying to memorize each card as you turn it over. When all seven are face-up, quickly turn them over. Then repeat, out loud as many of the cards as you can remember as speedily as you can. Now move those cards into a stack and place it beside the first stack. Do not mix the stacks together.

Repeat the same exercise with nine new cards, recalling as many as you can as fast as you can. Again don't worry if you don't remember them all, because it is unlikely you will unless you have a super incredible memory. Of course you will in time. Turn the cards over, place into a stack and move this stack of nine cards beside the other two stacks. Now the test:

Write down on a piece of paper as many of the five cards from the first stack as you can remember. Then, on a separate line, write down as many of the cards from the second stack (of seven) as you can remember. Then, on a third line write down as many of the last stack (nine cards) as you can remember. Do not write down more than the number of cards that were in the respective stack. To determine your score add up the number of cards you remembered from

Brain Exercise #6 (continued)

each stack by checking your answers against the stacks you put aside. For instance, let's say you remembered four in stack (line) one, five in stack two, six in stack three. Now multiply the total (in this case 15) by two (therefore, the first part of your score is 30). If you remembered a card, but couldn't remember which stack it was in and therefore wrote it down for the wrong stack, then obviously you do not count it as correct, yet (see below). You count only the cards remembered if they correspond with the stack they were in.

Next add up the total number of cards you correctly remembered in all the stacks, regardless of what stack they were in. In other words, you would count a card correct even if you paired it with the wrong stack, or row. Also, if you can't remember which stack a card was in but you definitely remember it was one of the cards in one of the stacks, just guess and put it in a row. However, do not put the card down more than once; that is, attribute it to two or three stacks. Otherwise you get no credit even if one of your guesses is the right row.

Now add up the total number correct out of all stacks. Then add this number to the first number (where you doubled the number that was associated with the correct answers in each, appropriate stack). This becomes your total score. Although you do get credit for remembering a card no matter which stack it appeared in, you get twice the credit (score) if you remember a card plus the stack it came from.

Brain Exercise #7 is very similar to the game "Concentration." However, it is played with a deck of cards.

These memory exercises will surely help build your memory for faces and names, where you parked your car, and much more. And, although you are instructed to recall or find the matched pair of cards as quickly as possible, these exercises are designed to actually increase your memory capacity, as well as your attention and recall speed. Remember, the faster your brain processes information, the faster you can learn and the better you can remember.

In conclusion, you can optimize your learning and memory skills by focusing 100 percent of your attention on what you want to learn, intending and committing to learn and remember it, providing the right nutritional environment

---

Brain Exercise #7
Memory Power Exercise

Pull 13 pairs of cards out of a deck of cards. For example, a 2 of spades and a 2 of hearts makes a pair; a Jack of clubs and a Jack of diamonds make a pair. Choose 13 pairs from twos all the way up to Aces. Now shuffle all 13 pairs (26 cards) and arrange them all face-up in five rows. Place five cards across in the top row, five across in the second row, six across in the third row, and five across in the fourth and fifth rows.

Now, set a timer for one minute and study and memorize where the matched pairs are in the deck until the timer goes off. Then turn over the cards, leaving them face-down in their same place in the grid. Write down what time it is when you begin this next part of the exercise. Start by turning over two cards in hopes of matching them. If you get a matched pair quickly pick them up and put them aside. If, however, the two are not matched, turn them back over and try again. Your objective is to find, turn over, and remove from the table all matched pairs until there are none left. Once you have done that, record what time it is. Your score on this is your time. Keep doing this exercise and try to improve your time. You can also challenge others in this brain exercise game, and compete against their time.

---

for your memory cells, and speed training your attention and thinking, and learning and memory brains.

Push-Ups Versus a Nautilus Machine

Everyone knows push-ups and chin-ups can build big strong muscles. Just look at those Olympic gymnasts on TV. However, the art and science of exercise technique and technology have evolved over the years to offer us Nautilus machines and other high-tech resistance training machines and techniques. The result is that you can build bigger, stronger muscles in significantly less time.

The same holds true for brain building. The above mentioned push-ups for your brain will help develop your memory, focus, and speed. But, not as fast or efficiently as my online brain speed exercises that harness the power of the computer's multi-megahertz processing speeds to measure your brain's processing speed.

> If you want to give your brain a real neuro-stimulating, brain power building workout try my brain speed exercise games at www.MyBrainTrainer.com/2020.

Benefits of Daily Brain Speed and Memory Exercise

- Warm up your brain for challenging day ahead
- Quick brain tune up for important meeting, creative session, exam
- Gain the mental edge for card game, tennis match, chess, etc.
- Develop long-term brainpower (speed and memory) improvements
- Stimulate growth of new brain cells and connections
- Have more mental energy, clarity and focus
- Look and feel quicker, smarter, sharper
- Preserve and protect your brain cells

Now remember, as small as it is, your brain is the most metabolically active clump of cells in your body, demanding as much as half of the energy nutrients, such as glucose in your blood under peak mental loads. Your brain never stops working. It is always there for you. Thinking, calculating, planning, comparing, deciding, directing — your brain's work is never done. And, in the same way that a high-performance car engine will not run very well without the right kind of fuel, your high-performance brain won't run without the right fuel either. That's why the real question we all should be asking ourselves every day is, "What am I going to feed my brain today?" In the next chapter you are going to find all the answers you need to that question. You are about to learn how to satisfy Neural Number Two — neural nutrition.

8

Food for Thought…Literally

"…a mind, if given only the best food never craves any other."

Rheta Childe Dorr

Research has established that in a very good way the nutrients in certain foods go right to your head, bringing with them fabulous brain health and fitness-enhancing effects. Amazingly, many of these nutrients can significantly, even dramatically, improve your brain speed and mental performance. You can use smart nutrition to protect your brain from the damaging effects of harmful free radicals and inflammation, and even offset the accumulated damage that has built up over the years. Even more remarkable — most of these brain-essential foods are all right at your fingertips.

You learned in Chapter 5 that the world you live in can be hard on your brain. There are many things your brain is exposed to each day that you have no control over. But you do have power over what you put into your mouth. In fact, much of what you are about to learn is going to empower you to make smarter food choices every day – food choices that are going to boost your brainpower and protect your precious brain cells from harm.

You've Got To Have Fat — Brain-Essential Fat That Is

All forms of communication and nutrient exchange that go on in your brain depend on the health and tone of the lipid bi-layer, the fatty membrane surrounding your brain cells. This spandex-like structure provides the protection, permeability, and flexibility necessary for the transportation of information, nutrition, electrons, and waste in and out of every cell, and from one cell to the next, quickly and efficiently. In order for this membrane to stay healthy, fluid, and flexible your diet must contain a balance of what I call brain-essential fats. Without them your brain's speed, health, and fitness can suffer significantly.

Essential fatty acids (EFAs) are those your body does not make. You need to get them from your diet or from supplements. Brain-essential fatty acids are vital to the structure and function of your brain. They are what I call smart fats and are predominantly grouped in two categories. The Omega-3s come predominantly from fish, nuts, and eggs. The Omega-6s come from sunflower, corn, sesame, and soy oils. Balancing your intake of these two groups is critical to optimum brain health and performance, for the rest of your life. When you have enough of them in your diet, your brain can continually renew and rebuild itself.

A healthy brain needs close to a 2:1 ratio of Omega-6s to 3s. Unfortunately, the modern American diet is severely out of balance when it comes to these important brain-essential fats. Due to excessive consumption of 6s and low consumption of 3s, the ratio is often as high as 20:1. Nothing causes brain cells to slow down, or age, faster than this imbalance. Not to worry, you can balance your Omega-3s and 6s quite easily.

Docosahexaenoic acid, or DHA, is an Omega-3 fatty acid that your brain cannot live or perform without. It is a principal component of your brain cell membrane. It is so important that if it is not abundantly present when you are in your mother's womb your brain development can become compromised. What's more, recent studies have shown that inadequate DHA in your diet can result in poor cognitive performance later in life. Along with Eicosapentaenoic acid (EPA) another Omega-3, DHA helps regulate many hormones, reduce oxidative stress and inflammation; it also lowers insulin resistance, triglycerides, depression, and arthritic pain. DHA also helps to buffer the negative effects of Arachidonic Acid, which you learned about in Chapter 5. DHA has been shown to improve memory, mood, mental quickness, and attention. The best source of DHA is fish, especially salmon, tuna, mackerel, halibut, trout, sardines, lox, anchovies, and herring.

Alpha linolenic acid (ALA) is another important Omega-3 essential fatty acid. It is an important precursor of DHA and EPA, but the conversion process is inefficient — 100 grams of ALA makes only about one gram of DHA. ALA has been shown to lower cholesterol, blood pressure, and possibly arterial and cerebral plaques. How do you get enough ALA in your diet? Eat walnuts, pumpkin and flaxseeds, eggs, and cold-pressed flax, walnut, hemp, and pumpkin seed oils.

Like the Omega-3s, phospholipids are also vitally important to your brain. They are found in high concentrations in practically every cell in your body, including brain cells. Phospholipids in the brain cell membranes help control the minerals, nutrients, and drugs that are transported in and out of brain cells. They also help brain cells communicate with each other. Two of the most important phospholipids are phosphatidyl choline (PC) and phosphatidyl serine (PS).

PC plays many important roles in your brain. It is a basic constituent of cellular membranes, and a major constituent of the myelin sheath that protects your nerve fibers, or axons. It is also necessary for the synthesis of your brain's speed molecule acetylcholine — the learning, remembering, and thinking neurotransmitter. It also protects vulnerable brain cells against lipid oxidation, one of the most damaging forms of oxidative stress. PC has been shown to improve memory and attention, and lower depression. PC is found in soy products such as lecithin, and in fish, peanuts, and egg yolks.

Phosphatidyl serine is another very important membrane component reported to improve memory, and enhance the sensitivity of the hypothalamus-pituitary-adrenal axis, thereby down-regulating stress-induced cortisol production and reducing its damaging effects on brain cells. PS has received FDA approval for cognitive enhancement claims. PC and PS are both available in supplemental capsules and powder, and I will discuss more about taking them in that form in Chapter 10.

When you incorporate enough brain-essential oils, fats, and fatty acids into your diet, you give your brain what it needs to maintain peak performance. Messages and memories are communicated swiftly and efficiently.

Protein – Your Thoughts Depend On It

Protein provides your body with the amino acids it needs to build cells, repair tissue, and defend against invading bacteria and viruses. In your brain, amino acids are the building blocks of your neurotransmitters — the chemical messengers that transport messages from one cell to another. Perception, learning, memory, and emotions all require neurotransmission. Without sufficient brain-essential amino acids, concentration, mood, and memory can fade fast.

Tyrosine is an amino acid found in protein. It can also be synthesized in the body from phenylalanine, another amino acid found in most protein foods. Tyrosine is the building block of norepinephrine and dopamine, the neurotransmitters in charge of alertness, coordination, physical activity, and focus. Norepinephrine, your brain's form of adrenaline, keeps you alert during times of need, pressure, or a fight for survival. It also helps you form new memories and place them in long-term storage. Dopamine is also important for alertness and focus, as well as proper immune and nervous system function. It also helps motivate you. Without enough dopamine in your brain you might find it difficult to assert yourself. Dopamine can be depleted by stress, excess sugar, alcohol, and caffeine. Tyrosine, a primary precursor of dopamine, is abundant in tuna, turkey, ricotta and cottage cheese, nonfat milk powder, oats and oatmeal, and beans, especially soybeans. It is also found in chicken, beef, and wild rice.

Tryptophan is the amino acid that helps your brain make serotonin, the neurotransmitter that allows you to feel contentment and satisfaction, to relax, and to sleep peacefully at night. Serotonin helps regulate mood and memory, as well as appetite and body temperature. Low serotonin almost always accompanies depression, sleep problems, and excessive stress hormones and thus impaired memory. Tuna, turkey, cottage cheese, soybeans, and oats are rich in tryptophan. Grains, spinach, chicken, fish, and soy milk are also high in this important brain-essential amino acid.

Recent studies have shown that bioactive peptides and proteins in milk, as well as minerals, such as calcium and magnesium, seem to improve factors related to Metabolic Syndrome – blood pressure, LDL and HDL cholesterol levels, obesity, and insulin resistance. Since Metabolic Syndrome is considered to be a prediabetic stage, and since it has also been associated with impaired cognitive function, often maligned milk, especially low-fat milk, might actually be a good source of brain-essential protein and minerals for your brain.

The Carb Secret...Brain Energy and Protection

Your brain cells have a sweet tooth, it's true. They love the energy that comes with a good sugar rush. In moments of peak mental performance your brain can demand up to half the glucose in your bloodstream. It is a sugar addict for sure. With little or no glucose your sugar-loving brain cells would literally shrivel up and die. So, in spite of all the hoopla over low-carb diets, carbohydrates are essential for optimal mental performance, focus, and especially brain speed. Of course I am not talking about just any carbohydrates, I am talking about low-glycemic, complex carbohydrates. In your body, these good-for-your-brain carbs take longer to convert into blood sugar because of their complex structure and fiber content.

The Glycemic Index (GI) was established to define the blood sugar impact commensurate with eating specific carbohydrates. Study participants were given 50 grams of glucose to consume. The subsequent rise in their blood sugar, which was quick and plentiful, created the reference number of 100. In other words, glucose has a glycemic index of 100. A carbohydrate that results in half the sugar rush of glucose ranks as 50 on the glycemic index. Table 8.1 illustrates the difference between high- and low-glycemic carbohydrates.

Glycemic Index (GI)

HIGH (above 50)

Honey	55
Watermelon, pineapple, cantaloupe, raisins, bananas	55-75
Instant and white rice, baguette, rice cakes	70-100
Soft drinks, fruit drinks, mixed alcoholic drinks	70+
Bread (except pumpernickel and sprouted grains)	70+
Cereals (except bran and oatmeal)	70-90
Cookies and crackers	70+
Bagels, croissants, waffles, donuts, chips	70+
Parsnip, potatoes, pumpkin, beets	70-100
Candy	70-85
Table sugar	75
Dates	100

Glycemic Index (GI)

LOW (below 50)

Nuts (walnuts, almonds, peanuts)	15-20
Beans (black, red, kidney)	20-40
Fruit – cherries, grapefruit, apple,	25-40
Vegetables	20-40
Whole grains, basmati rice	30-45
Berries and grapes	40-50
Brown rice	50

Table 8.1

You can protect your brain and avoid blood sugar crashes by maintaining a carbohydrate balance that is no more than 40 to 50 percent of your total caloric intake, eating carbs that are below 50 on the glycemic index. The rule of thumb for maintaining steady brain energy is to try to keep the GI average of all the carbs you eat at any one meal under 50. That means if you have only one carb on your plate, it should be under 50. If you have two or more carbs their combined GIs should average out to 50 or below. Don't worry, you will learn much more about this in the next chapter, and I will give you plenty of meal suggestions to help you out.

Energy for brain cells is not the only reason that certain carbohydrates are so essential to your brain. Many complex carbohydrates also contain powerful brain-capillary-, membrane-, and mitochondria-protecting antioxidants. These neuroprotective properties are derived from the polyphenolic compounds, primarily flavonoids, found in a broad range of fruits, vegetables, legumes, herbs, and other plants, and grains (Table 8.2).

Flavonoids, such as quercetin, catechin, resveratrol, anthocyanidins, and proanthocyanidins have been scientifically shown to possess powerful brain-protecting antioxidant and anti-inflammatory effects. So powerful are their effects (estimated to be up to 50 to 100 times stronger than vitamin E), that they can protect brain cells, membranes, mitochondria, and even DNA from the devastating effects of free radical-induced oxidative damage. They also strengthen and protect the delicate cerebral vascular blood vessels from inflammation and the occlusions

Protective Brain-Essential Carbs

Carbohydrate Source Glycemic Index (GI)	Active Ingredient(s)	Function
Blueberries, or dark skinned berries, grapes and plums GI less than 50	Anthocyanidins, quercetin and resveratrol in skin Proanthocyanidins in seeds	Powerful antioxidant. Anti-inflammatory. Increases cell signaling. Promotes mental performance.
Greens plus sweet potato, squash, tomato GI 20-50	Carotenoids (beta-carotene)	Powerful antioxidant
Red wine GI 50 plus	Anthocyandins, proanthocyanidins, and resveratrol (Res)	Powerful antioxidants Res blocks lipid peroxidation and inhibits COX2 inflammatory markers
Spinach, kale, avocado. GI less than 30	Lutein, folic acid	Multiple neuroprotective factors
Tomato and sauces, red bell pepper. GI less than 30. Watermelon. GI greater than 50	Lycopene	Neuroprotective
Avocado. GI less than 30	Glutathione, lutein, folic acid, monounsaturated fat (oleic acid)	Powerful neuroprotection and immune enhancing effects
Apples, broccoli, cabbage, onions. GI less than 40	Quercetin	May protect against Alzheimer's. Powerful antioxidant. Anti-inflammatory. Increase norepenephrine

Table 8.2

that can block the flow of vital nutrients to your forever-hungry brain. Two flavonoids — catechin and quercetin — were recently shown to lower the risk of Alzheimer's and to increase norepinephrine production in the brain. This results in better oxidation (burning) of fats and increased energy levels within the brain. And, the carotenoids, such as beta-carotene, lutein, and lycopene are also powerful antioxidants that protect the brain against the ravages of free radicals. Apples, asparagus, avocados, cabbage, garlic, onions, tomatoes, red bell peppers, beets, carrots, yams, squash, and sweet potatoes are all great and brainy carbs.

The key to sustainable peak mental performance is making sure your brain blood sugar supply is adequate and steady; that brain-essential fatty acids are plentifully in your diet; and that you are getting an abundance of brain-essential amino acids from the best proteins. So how do you get enough of all the right brain-essential foods in your diet? Actually, it is pretty simple. All you have to do is eat as many of the following foods, as often as you can.

20/20 Brain Power Must-Have Foods

FABULOUS FISH: Fish and fish oil supplements should become staples in your diet. They are rich in the brain-essential Omega-3 fatty acid DHA. Cold-water, wild fish are best, especially salmon, sardines, herring, mackerel, and tuna. Deep water fish are less polluted with mercury, dioxins, and other toxins. Farmed fish are not as high in brain-essential fatty acids and the waters they are raised in are often loaded with bacteria and other harmful contaminants. Try to have at least three fabulous fish choices a week.

BRAINY BERRIES: Antioxidant rich blueberries, raspberries, blackberries, strawberries, cranberries, and dark-skinned grapes are a must in a brain-essential diet. Eat them every day. When buying berries, fresh are always best, but frozen will do in the off-season. Wild blueberries have a higher concentration of brain-essential antioxidants. In government-sponsored studies at Tufts University, researchers fed blueberries, spinach, strawberries, and vitamin E to rats. The rats were then tested for balance, memory, and speed while navigating a maze. Within a very short time the rats were performing like young rats again, with those eating blueberries at the head of the pack.

BRILLIANT BEANS: Beans for your brain? Absolutely. Beans may be the perfect brain food. These low-glycemic carbs also contain protein, fiber, and brain-essential amino acids. And, dark beans like black, red, and red kidney also have high levels of antioxidants. Red and white kidney beans can even help to lower the glycemic effect of other starchy carbohydrates in your meal because of their phaseolamin content. Phaseolamin is a starch-blocker that naturally inhibits amylase, the pancreatic enzyme that helps your body digest starches. Starchy foods such as rice or potatoes convert to glucose rapidly. Phaseolamin naturally slows down this process, and prevents insulin levels from rising rapidly. Soybeans, and products made from them such as tofu, tempeh, and soy milk are also great sources of lecithin and isoflavones.

WISE WALNUTS: Take a look at a walnut. What does it look like? That's right, it looks like a brain. Maybe Mother Nature had a plan when she created this magnificent nut. A handful of walnuts, approximately two ounces, contains almost three grams of Omega-3s. Moreover, walnuts, along with peanuts, pecans, and hazelnuts are very high in brain-protecting antioxidants. When shopping for walnuts it is best to buy them in the shell because their valuable oils are still protected. If you are buying walnut halves, try to taste them first to make sure they are not rancid. Avoid walnut pieces as their oils have likely gone south.

Pumpkin, flax, hemp, and chia seeds also provide Omega-3s. Hemp seeds have an almost perfect 3:1 ratio of Omega-6s to 3s, and they make great-tasting oil. You can find hemp oil in most health food stores. Extra virgin olive oil and cold-pressed flax, hemp, walnut, and pumpkin seed oils are produced with a low-heat, cold-press extraction process that maintains the integrity and nutritive value of the oil. Olive oil can help neutralize the effects of other bad brain fats that have accumulated in your lipid membranes. Olive oil also has a positive effect on lowering insulin resistance.

EGGHEAD EGGS: Eggs are perfect brain protein, and more. They are rich in lecithin or phosphatidyl choline. Lecithin, which is great for your brain membranes, is also a great natural emulsifier of fat and cholesterol. That means it can help manage and down-regulate the amount of bad fat and cholesterol that actually gets into your bloodstream. In fact, scientific studies have shown that lecithin can lower blood cholesterol levels. Eggs are also rich in lipids, phosphatidyl choline, serine, inositol, and the all-important brain-essential aminos tyrosine and tryptophan.

Eggs have gotten bad press over the years because they contain cholesterol. If you are concerned about cholesterol, check with your doctor about including eggs in your diet. However, keep in mind cholesterol is very necessary in the body. In fact, your liver manufactures significantly more than you would get from an egg or two. Cholesterol helps insulate the nerve fibers that are a key component of the important myelin sheath that surrounds your axons. Cholesterol also helps maintain healthy brain cell membranes. In addition, cholesterol in food does not automatically turn into cholesterol that can clog your arteries. Remember, when purchasing eggs you want organic eggs that come from free-range chickens. Most of these advertise on the label that they are high in Omega-3 or DHA, the brain-essential fatty acid found almost exclusively in certain fish.

COGNITIVE CHEESE: Low-fat cottage and ricotta cheeses are rich in brain-essential amino acids, especially tyrosine. Tyrosine helps your brain make those important neurotransmitters, such as dopamine, for mental energy and focus, as well as sexual energy. Cottage cheese is a great snack protein for a brain energy pickup. Topped with berries, walnuts, and/or freshly ground flaxseeds, it is a delicious — and quick — breakfast, lunch, or snack. However, try to eat cottage cheese before eating any high-glycemic carbs, like bread or fruit juice. A heightened level of blood sugar can block the transport of tyrosine across the blood-brain barrier. This then allows tryptophan to enter the brain first, which causes your brain to produce serotonin, thus taking away that mental edge you may want to preserve during your workday.

SAGACIOUS SPINACH: Popeye may have been onto something. He loved Olive Oyl and he ate lots and lots of spinach. Maybe that is why he always outsmarted Brutus and Bluto. Spinach ranks at the top of the list of brain foods. It actually protects healthy brain cells and rejuvenates the old and tired ones. Maybe it is the high level of folic acid in the spinach leaves. Folic acid is a powerful neuroprotective member of the B vitamin family. A typical vitamin B100 tablet contains 400 mcg. of folic acid. You should get more. Eating lots of spinach will help. One highly studied group of Alzheimer's-resistant nuns revealed substantial amounts of folic acid foods in their diet. Spinach also has chlorophyll and lutein, as well as powerful flavonoids which provide long-lasting antioxidant protection to your brain.

Other greens, such as arugula, kale, broccoli, basil, cilantro, watercress, and sea vegetables such as kelp, dulse, and the dark green algae, spirulina, are also great for brain speed, health, and fitness.

BRAIN SPICE OF LIFE: Did you know that even some of the spices in your kitchen contain powerful phytonutrients that can boost memory and reduce inflammation, free radicals, and oxidative damage to the brain? Well, they can. For example, curcumin, a member of the ginger family, is the active ingredient found in the bright yellow spice turmeric (also found in curry). Studies show that it is so powerful it may not only help prevent Alzheimer's, it may actually reverse the beta-amyloid plaque buildup that many believe cause the memory loss and cognitive dysfunction characteristic of the disease. Ginger, also great to cook with, has very similar effects. Cinnamon is another powerful spice. Just the scent has been shown to improve memory. Cinnamon also improves cellular utilization of glucose, which helps lower glucose intolerance and insulin resistance, two devastating contributors to cognitive decline. It is great added to coffee, apple pie, and other desserts. Rosemary, sage, and lemon balm have also been shown to improve cognitive function while reducing the harmful effects of free radicals in the brain. Cilantro, the parsley-like green herb so popular in salsa and other Mexican dishes, has been found to chelate, or remove, mercury from your cells. Use all of these spices as regularly as you can to help perk up and protect your brain.

Burning Bright

At the beginning of this chapter we talked about the importance of the right fuel in a high-performance engine. Now you have learned what kind of foods can properly fuel your high-performance brain. But that is not the end of the brain-essential food story. You see, when it comes to your brain, it is not only the foods you eat that matters, it is when you eat them, too. When the fuel ratios are not right in your car you get pinging in the engine. When your brain-essential food ratios are not right you get pinging in your head — your mind gets fuzzy and forgetful.

In the next chapter you are going to learn how to combine your brain-essential foods in just the right ratios to provide your brain with the nutrition and energy it needs to be as sharp as possible, all day long.

9

Neuro-Nutrition

The Art and Science of Brain Speed Nutrition

When health is absent, wisdom cannot reveal itself, art cannot manifest, strength cannot fight, wealth becomes useless, and intelligence cannot be applied.

Herophilus

When you think about eating from now on you may want to think about feeding your head and not your stomach. Most certainly, what you eat can highly influence your brain's performance level, as well as health and fitness. I like to think of it as better thinking through better brain chemistry. But that is only part of the brain fuel equation. To your brain, it is not just what you eat that is important, but how you eat it, and when.

Your brain requires the right glucose-to-amino-to-lipid ratio so it can run lean and clean all day long. How you mix your brain-essential carbs, fats, and proteins determines how and when certain nutrients get to your brain. For example, if protein is eaten before carbohydrates then the brain-essential amino acid tyrosine gets to your brain cells quickly. Tyrosine insures lots of high-performance brainpower – something you want during the day. If you get adequate tyrosine in the morning and early afternoon your brain is going to be awake and active for your workday. On the other hand, in the evening you want your brain to get mostly tryptophan. Remember, tryptophan can help you unwind. It has a calming effect on your hard-working brain. When you consume high-glycemic carbs such as potatoes, rice, bread, or pasta first they quickly turn into blood sugar, which helps transport tryptophan across the blood-brain barrier. Just be mindful, even nighttime carb consumption still requires moderation.

My 20/20 Brain Power food ratios are designed to optimize your mental energy and sharpness during the day, and then help you relax and sleep at night. These food group ratios are modeled around the latest research in fat-to-carb-to-protein ratio required to maximize weight loss, increase lean muscle mass (with exercise, of course), and promote optimal energy and overall health. My ratios follow the basic 40/30/30, carbs-to-proteins-to-fats rule. However, I very tightly define those food groups as follows:

1. Carbs – 40 percent or less of total meal calories. Maintain an average GI (glycemic index) below 50 or carb impact below 20. You will learn more about carb impact shortly. The majority of your carbs should come from foods rich in antioxidants, flavonoids and carotenoids — berries, grapes, and apples, beans, greens, red bell peppers, tomatoes, yams, squash, cabbage, carrots, and onions – there are lots to choose from.

2. Protein – 30 percent of total meal calories (up to 50 percent at breakfast). Your proteins should be derived from fresh, wild fish, organic poultry, tofu, eggs, and low-fat dairy such as cottage or ricotta cheese, milk, and yogurt. Good secondary protein sources include nuts and beans. Try to limit your intake of red meats, most of which are high in brain-draining saturated fats and cholesterol.

3. Fats – 30 percent of total meal calories. Fats should be derived mainly from fish, nuts, seeds and extra-virgin olive oil. Avoid trans fats — margarines, commercial salad and cooking oils, fried foods, and baked goods such as bagels, cookies, and cakes, like the plague.

20/20 Brain Power Carb-to-Protein Rules

- Proteins before carbs for breakfast
- Proteins before carbs for snacks and lunch
- Carbs before proteins for dinner

Playing Your Carbs Just Right

A steady flow of the right amount of blood sugar to your brain can fuel your neurons, and give you exactly what you need to stay sharp, focused, and at the peak of your game. That is why it is important to understand the ups and downs of eating carbohydrates. In the last chapter you learned about high- and low-glycemic carbs. Now you are going to learn how to combine them to give your brain the nice, steady flow of sugar it needs to thrive.

High- and low-glycemic carbs can balance each other out when they are eaten together at the same meal. For example, you can have a potato (GI 70+) for lunch as long as you also have an equivalent amount of low-GI carbs such as broccoli, cauliflower, cabbage, beans, or tomatoes, or a salad with a GI under 30, of course. At lunch you still want to have your proteins before your carbs, unless you are enjoying those nice, low-glycemic carbs that do not rapidly convert to blood sugar. If that is the case you are almost certain to derive the energy-boosting effects of tyrosine from your protein. At dinner it all reverses. Now you want to eat those tasty, high-glycemic carbs first. Not only do you get to eat some of those tasty, rich carbs that you have been thinking about all day, you can even have a little red wine and a sweet if you choose. This is pure neurochemistry. These yummy foods can help you feel relaxed, happy, and ready for a good night's sleep.

Sounds pretty simple, doesn't it? And it is. But let's take this whole carb lesson another step further. The reason that eating low-glycemic carbs and balancing high-glycemic carbs with low is so important is this: it protects you from sugar surges.

Nothing is as important to your brain as modulating the blood sugar impact of your meals. Sugar surges right after a meal, as well as the elevated insulin levels that they cause, do the most damage to your brain. Eating high-glycemic carbs (bread, sweets, cereals, rice, and potatoes) produces an almost immediate rush of sugar into your bloodstream. This is followed by an equivalent surge of insulin, which leads to a blood sugar crash, wild energy and mood swings, and mental fog. Over time, glucose intolerance and insulin resistance set in. This sets the stage for a steep decline in brainpower and ultimately the demise of your vulnerable brain cells.

When you are required by a doctor to have your blood sugar level assessed, the test is usually done in the morning after you have fasted overnight. Although these tests do reflect your waking blood sugar levels they do not reveal the blood sugar impact of the carbs you consumed at the meal you ate the night before. Technically this is called the glycemic load of a meal. I call it the carb impact. A high carb impact means a fast and furious release of sugar into the blood. Table 9.1 is a handy reference guide for the carb impact of some of our favorite foods.

To determine the glycemic load of a food, its glycemic index (GI) is multiplied by the amount of carbohydrates in grams that it provides and then that number is divided by 100. Essentially, every unit of a food's glycemic load is equivalent to the blood glucose-raising effect of 1 gram of pure glucose or white bread. One medium apple, for example, that weighs 120 grams has a glycemic index of 38. It provides 15 grams of carbohydrates, therefore its glycemic load or carb impact is 6. This means the carb impact is low, and that's good. A bagel, on the other hand, has a carb impact above 25. This is because the average 3- to 4-ounce bagel is made of very starchy, high-glycemic flour. A carb impact of 25 is almost equal to your entire carb allotment for a meal. That's not good.

Your goal, if you want to protect and preserve your brain, is to keep the total load, or carb impact of a snack or meal under 30, especially in your breakfast and lunch meals. For dinner, you are allowed to splurge on carbs, a little.

Understanding and using these carb-impact guidelines can help you in several ways. First it allows you to indulge in a sweet or high-glycemic treat if your meal portion is relatively small, such as a teaspoon or two of honey, or a small scoop of ice cream. And, it prevents you from being lulled into eating a large portion of a relatively low-GI carb, such as spaghetti or white rice in the typical portion of four to six ounces. In this case the starchy carb has a higher glycemic load, or impact, on your blood sugar and insulin than several teaspoons of sugar.

Carb Impact Food Chart			
Group 1 Low-Impact Below 10	Group 2 Medium-Impact between 10-20	Group 3 High-Impact Above 20	Group 4 High-Impact Snacks (20+)
Apple	Banana	Baked Beans	Alcoholic Drinks
Asparagus	Beets	Cereals (except bran and oats)	Bagel
Avocado	Corn		Baguette
Artichoke	Fruit Juices (apple, berry, pineapple)	Couscous	Candy (fruit bars the highest)
Barley		French Fries	
Beans	Hi-Amylose rice	Macaroni and Cheese	Chips
Bran Cereal	Honey (2 tsp)		Cookies
Bread (1 slice)	Ice Cream (scoop)	Pancakes	Crackers
Broccoli	Mango	Pizza	Croissant
Cereal	Oatmeal (not instant)	Potato, Baked	Potato Chips
Cabbage		Rice Pudding	Pretzels
Cauliflower	Orange Juice (6oz.)	Rice Noodles	Rice Cake
Garlic	Papaya	Tapioca	Soft Drinks
Juices (tomato, V- 8, grapefruit)	Pineapple	White Pasta	
	Rice (Basmati, whole-grain brown)	White Rice	
Kale			
Nuts	Spaghetti (whole wheat)		
Onions			
Peas	Sweet Potato		
Red Bell Pepper	Yams		
Sea Green	Jell-O		
Spinach			
Soy Milk			
Squash			
Tomato			
Zucchini			

Table 9.1

Group One low-impact carb servings have very few calories, do not raise insulin levels, and in some cases may even help to lower insulin resistance. Group Two carb servings are relatively neutral; that is, they won't raise blood sugar levels too fast. Group Three high-impact carbs, when eaten without an equal or greater amount of low-GI carbs, tend to raise blood sugar and insulin levels quickly. Group Four high-impact snack carbs are the carbs we munch on between meals, or have with a meal, such as a baguette. You know what they are. We all love them, but a little goes a very long way when it comes to your brain.

Even though super high-impact carbs are not good for your brain, sometimes you just have to have one. And you can. But keep this in mind. When you do have that Kaiser Roll or baguette, you are not only piling on the calories, you are piling on the sugar and insulin. That means you could be headed for a bad brain day. Not good if you need all your wits about you for an important meeting at work or a special occasion. But if you do have to have that bread, balance it out. Have it with protein: a poached egg, a piece of salmon, a slice of lox, a turkey patty, or peanut butter, even some low-fat cottage cheese. And eat the protein first. It is so much better for your brain.

I need to take a moment here to address the issue of how many calories are good for the brain. A solid and growing base of scientific research shows that aging, and especially brain aging, slow down when calories are restricted by 30 to 40 percent. Calorie restriction (CR) not only seems to almost stop aging, it can reverse mental decline, boost brainpower, even intelligence and physical strength, all while improving overall health. CR can even reverse the expression of several diseases that typically start later in life.

A normal daily calorie intake for women is approximately 2,100 to 2,200 calories or 2,400 to 2,600 for men, assuming an average weight of 155 pounds. The CR diet range is approximately 1,300 to 1,400 calories for women and 1,500 to 1,600 for men. Unfortunately, most of us are not yet willing to cut back that much on our food intake. Quite fortunately, however, we may be able to slow down our metabolic and cellular aging rate by lowering the carb impact of the foods we eat. In other words, a diet rich in low-impact carbs may be metabolically and biochemically the same to the body as a calorie-restricted diet, even though its total calorie intake may fall in the normal range of 2,100 or 2,500 calories per day.

The 20/20 Brain Power Plate

Counting calories is no fun; in fact, it can stress out your brain. That is why I am not asking you to do it. Instead, at each meal you are simply going to divide your plate into sections, like a pizza or pie plate. The number of sections varies at each meal. You will be putting your protein in one of the sections and your carbs in the others.

You can estimate your protein requirement, typically three to four ounces of protein food per meal. You can use your hand as a measuring reference. Your protein portion should be about the same in thickness and volume as the palm of your hand. For an average 155-pound person the protein portion is about the size of a deck of cards, or a quarter-pound burger. If you are heavier, have a little more; if you are lighter a little less. This is in addition to the protein you might get in certain carbs. Beans, nuts, and dairy are secondary sources of protein. Count your protein from primary protein sources only.

Carbs are chosen from each of the four Carb Impact groups. Keep in mind that they can balance each other out. If you eat a carb that is high with an equal portion of carbs that are low, you average your Carb Impact for that meal. For example, if you eat white rice you can balance out its impact with an equivalent portion of brain-healthy veggies. There are also other ways to lower the glycemic impact of your carbs. These include having fiber, fat or oil, and/or something acetic such as vinegar, wine, or lemon juice with your meal. These have all been shown to prolong the conversion time of carbohydrates into blood sugar.

So, what about fat? As long as you derive a majority of your fat, that is essential fatty acids, from fish, seeds and nuts, and olive oil, and you stay away from fried foods, supermarket salad and cooking oils, and red meat, you don't need to worry about counting fat calories, at least for the 20 day program. More important – you must absolutely stay completely away from the trans fats (fried fast foods, baked goods, and most salad oils), and keep to a minimum those saturated, animal, and dairy fats. That means go with low or no fat milk, cottage cheese, and yogurt.

Now let's get specific and start plating your meals the 20/20 Brain Power way.

Breakfast

Breakfast is when you establish your brain's metabolic set point for the rest of the day. Your whole brain day begins with breakfast. When you limit your carbs at breakfast, you have more brainpower for the rest of the day. For example, a breakfast of toast, bagels, croissants, or hash browns and a 6- to 8-ounce glass of orange juice, or a sugar-coated cereal with bananas is not going to carry your brain through the day. In fact, you could be headed for a mind slump that could last into the night.

Breakfast Possibilities

Your best choices for breakfast are proteins that are high in tyrosine — ricotta or cottage cheese, turkey, peanut butter, eggs, lox (smoked salmon), turkey/chicken sausage, oats, tofu and soy breakfast "meats," and beans.

Most of us don't think of beans for breakfast. However, from south of the border comes a truly brainy meal – the heady Huevos Rancheros. Huevos are not only good for brainpower, they are rich, yummy, and fulfilling, too. When you have beans for breakfast eat them with some straight protein like eggs, breakfast meats, or cottage cheese. And eat the protein before any bread, juice, or other high-glycemic carbs. If you don't, the carbs can block the transporters that escort tyrosine across the blood-brain barrier to your needy dopamine receptors. This opens the door for tryptophan to slip in and there goes your brain energy, mental acuity, and focus.

Here is a great idea for a great brainpower breakfast: One or two poached eggs (brain-essential aminos and lipids), on bed of spinach (raw, sautéed or lightly steamed), and a whole-grain, lard-free, organic corn tortilla (or toasted slice of whole-grain sprouted bread). Sprinkle on cayenne (red pepper), salsa, and parsley or cilantro, or both. You can round it off with a section or two of a grapefruit or an orange. You can even have a brain breakfast dessert of berries on plain low-fat yogurt. Now that is a very brainy beginning for your day.

If you are on the run, and you need something fast, one of my quick brainpower breakfast favorites is cottage cheese topped with walnuts and pumpkin seeds. Or add grapes, grapefruit slices, melon, or your favorite fruit. Sliced avocado is yummy and very brain healthy. Even chopped tomatoes are good. Sprinkle on a little flax meal (freshly ground flaxseeds) and enjoy a half-glass of orange,

BREAKFAST

20/20 Brain Food Ratio rules:
1. Divide your plate into TWO sections.
2. Fill one-half the plate with your Protein.
3. Fill the other half with Carbs from Group 1, or 1 and 2 only (sorry but no Group 3 carbs for breakfast).
4. If you slip up and just have to have a Group 3 (such as a potato cake) or even a Group 4 snack carb (maybe a bagel), balance it with at least an equal amount of carbs from Groups 1.
5. Have your protein before your carbs.
6. Try to have at least one of the primary 20/20 Brain Power foods.
7. Enjoy!

grapefruit, tomato, or V-8 juice. Another one of my on-the-run favorites is peanut butter (high in brain-healthy monounsaturated fats and antioxidants) and blueberry jam on a piece of toasted sprouted-grain bread. It is not only scrumptious, it is smart — the flavanoids in the dark berries have been shown to reverse signs of brain aging.

My absolute favorite breakfast on the run is a brainpower protein shake. Try my Berry Brainy Smoothie (see 20/20 Brain Power Recipe Book) with special tasty, yet powerful, brain nutrients. They deliver enough high-energy neuro-nutrients (which work even better if you exercise your brain or body first) to keep your brain in a steady high-performance mode for the rest of the day.

A special note about juices: blueberry, Concord grape, pomegranate, grapefruit, or cranberry juices are best, but only four to six ounces if they are high in sugar (over 24 grams per 8-ounce serving). Most fruit juices have over 24 grams of sugar, many over 30. That is equivalent to more than five teaspoons of sugar. Tomato and V-8 are great for providing the remarkable cancer-, heart disease-, and brain degeneration-fighting lycopenes. If the listed sugar amount is over 10 percent of the total serving size, cut back. Typically an 8-ounce cup equals 240 ml, so if the label shows over 24 grams of sugar, that is 10 percent of the serving so you may want to back off, or just have half a cup.

Watch for high-fructose corn syrup and sugar, they are hidden throughout the foods you buy. Check labels. Your brain will thank you, over and over. And please refer to your 20/20 Brain Power Recipe Book for many more recipes and suggestions.

Lunch

You have probably learned from experience that if you are not careful, lunch is the one meal that can drop your brain into the soup for the rest of the day. That is because you either had the wrong brain food ratio or too many high-impact carbs for lunch. How you mix and manage your proteins and carbs at lunch is going to determine whether or not you renew your brain energy for the rest of your day.

As with breakfast, your brainpower lunch goal is to stabilize your blood sugar by eating low-glycemic carbs, and only after getting plenty of brain-essential aminos into your tummy first. On a daily basis, you want to establish your brainpower potential at breakfast and sustain it with lunch. Your protein portion can range from 50 percent down to 33 percent of your calories (1/2 to 1/3 of your plate). Experiment and see what ratio works best to keep your mental focus, clarity, and energy strong for the rest of the day.

Lunch Possibilities

A super brainpower lunch might include seared Ahi (or canned tuna) on bed of greens, spinach and mixed veggies, topped with a lemon juice-based dressing. You could enjoy fruit juice or water as a beverage, and mixed berries on plain low-fat yogurt for dessert (especially if you didn't have any berries at breakfast). Other

LUNCH

20/20 Brain Food Ratio rules:
1. Divide plate into thirds.
2. Fill 1/3 with proteins high in brain-essential aminos.
3. Divide the carb section into thirds (approximately).
4. Fill your carb sections with foods from Group 1, 1 and 2, or 1, 2 and 3 (no Group 4 carbs, yet).
5. Have your protein first.
6. Try to have at least two of the primary 20/20 Brain Power foods.
7. À vôtre santé!

good brain proteins for lunch are eggs (in an omelet or quiche), cottage cheese or ricotta cheese, tofu or tempeh and other soy meats, and chicken and turkey. Add red kidney beans for fiber, which can help slow the surge of glucose into your bloodstream following a meal.

Good brainpower lunch carbs include beans, especially white and red kidney, pinto, soy, and small red and black beans. Also good are lentils, brown rice (long-grain if possible), spinach, arugula and other leafy greens, broccoli, brussels sprouts, cabbage, asparagus, avocados, red bell peppers, yams, sweet potatoes, squash, and cauliflower. And don't forget those flavorful green herbs, basil and cilantro. You can enjoy berries for dessert, of course. Other fruit choices include pineapple, mango, papaya, guava, and kiwi because of their enzymes, which help you digest your protein. However, since they are high on the glycemic index, limit yourself to small portions, except at dinner.

It is best that you have only a few, if any, high-impact white carbs (potatoes, white rice, bread, crackers, cookies, donuts, bagels, or buns) at lunch. White carbs are out except for basmati or long-grain, high-amylose rice, cauliflower, white beans, and pasta (only _ serving). If you want a burger, try it on a bed of brown or basmati rice, or better yet spinach and mixed greens. Hold the bun, or at least discard half of it. A small portion of pasta is OK for lunch, but not as the bulk of your carb allotment. In fact, if you have any white carbs, balance them out with equal portions of low-glycemic carbs — beans, broccoli, spinach, salad, and so on.

Please refer to the 20/20 Brain Power Recipe Book for more recipes and suggestions.

Dinner

At dinnertime your day is ending. It is time to relax. Your brain has put in a great day. Like a muscle that has been taut all day long, now your brain wants to unwind. It is time to let it go out of focus, out of being on purpose, and let it stop striving so hard. You want to open up your mind to all the blessings of your life — your spouse, your kids, your friends, the dog, the cat — everything that really matters to you. That's right; it's time to let your brain have a little fun. At dinner you are going to let your brain cells enjoy a plentiful portion of carbs. This is their reward for putting in such a fine brainy and productive day. Yes, that might include some healthy red wine and a scrumptious little dessert.

DINNER

20/20 Brain Food Ratio rules:
1. Divide your plate into four sections (quarters).
2. Fill one section (_ of your plate) with protein.
3. Fill the rest of your plate with carbs from any and all Groups; however, you must balance Group 3 with Group 1 carbs.
4. Eat your sweet, starchy, white high-glycemic carbs first.
5. Try to have at least three of the primary 20/20 Brain Power foods.
6. Bon appétit!

Earlier in the day your goal was to get plenty of brain-essential tyrosine to your brain cells before the carbs and tryptophan. At night it is quite the opposite. Dinner carbs can help your brain produce serotonin, especially when they are followed by proteins rich in the amino acid tryptophan. Serotonin is the feel good neurotransmitter that helps you unwind. It helps you calm down so you can enjoy your evening and then drift easily off to sleep. So now is the time to have those mashed potatoes or that glass of wine, as long as you follow them up with some tryptophan-rich protein. Foods highest in tryptophan are tuna, turkey, chicken, soybeans, cottage cheese, oats, peanuts and almonds, beans, milk, and fish.

Best brain-essential dinner proteins include fish, turkey and chicken, as well as tofu and beans. Try to have plenty of greens along with your richer carbs. Spinach, broccoli, and mixed salad greens can always be made tasty. The best carbs at dinnertime are red, green, and orange. That means greens plus tomatoes and or red bell peppers, beets, carrots, sweet potatoes, yams, pumpkin, and squash. Wonderful! This is a scrumptious blend of carbs, proteins, and powerful antioxidants for your brain. For dessert try mixed berries, sautéed in Grand Marnier or orange juice, on top of a scoop of yogurt or even vanilla ice cream. Delicious! And, all those carbs will certainly help you sleep tight.

Remember, at dinner eat your high-glycemic carbs first. This means you can start your meal with a drink, a slice of baguette with a little butter or olive oil, potatoes or rice. Go for it. Just remember, don't have too rich of a meal or you will end up feeling a little dull or thickheaded. You can be sure it is equally hard on your heart and body.

Dinner Possibilities

Other dinner possibilities include broiled salmon on a bed of brown rice with steamed broccoli, salad, and berries with yogurt for dessert. One of my favorite dinners is red bell peppers stuffed with ground turkey, onions, garlic, and sunflower seeds. Top that with a blended sauce of olive oil, lemon juice, and sesame seed butter (aka Tahini) and you have a delicious, yet brain-calming meal. Another one of my favorites is tofu broiled in soy sauce, ginger and garlic, and mixed with dark beans and chopped tomatoes and green onions, and smothered in the above Tahini sauce.

If you enjoy stir-fry you will love this recipe. Sauté onions, ginger, and garlic in olive oil with a little of the delicious spice turmeric. Add some broccoli and chopped red bell peppers and keep stirring until the veggies are al dente. Then add some fresh spinach, cover, and lightly steam the spinach. Sprinkle with sesame or sunflower seeds and serve over a bed of rice (optional). Oh, this really tastes good and healthy with one of my brain-soothing sauces.

Please refer to the 20/20 Brain Power Recipe Book for many more breakfast, lunch and dinner suggestions.

A Word About Wine

Finally, in the evening you can have a little wine. But, keep it to no more than two glasses of a good red wine. This is not an endorsement to start drinking. There are other ways to get the same antioxidant benefits that are derived from the dark grape skins and seeds — a glass of Concord grape juice, for example. The anthocyanidins (from the skin) and proanthocyanidins (from the seeds) are indeed powerful neuroprotective agents, much stronger even than vitamin E. These two polyphenol flavonoid compounds are also enhanced synergistically by other powerful nutrients, such as quercetin and catechins found in green tea, ginkgo, blueberries, broccoli, onions, apples, and cabbage.

The real magic bullet in wine is now believed to be Resveratrol, or Res. It may be the answer to the French and Mediterranean Diet paradox — eating rich foods, lots of fat (all that olive oil), consuming generous amounts of all that wine, and living longer than most health-conscious Americans.

Res reportedly prevents, and maybe even reverses, cancer, heart disease, and brain dysfunction and decline. It is one of the most powerful antioxidants known, believed to be 50 to 100 times more powerful than vitamin E. It also squelches inflammation because it appears to be a COX-2 inhibitor, too. Best of all, Res really does guard your membranes, protecting them from bad brain fats and free radicals. It stops lipid peroxidation in its tracks. Your brain loves Res. The good news is Res is not just found in wine it is also found in peanuts, raspberries, mulberries, and certain dark-skinned grapes, such as the Muscatine variety.

OK, one last red wine story. Two recent studies have shown that red wine improves the blood sugar, blood coagulability, and antioxidant and lipid profiles after a meal. This is very surprising because almost every carb that is high on the glycemic index causes a postprandial (after meal) spike in glucose and subsequent surges in fatty acids, triglycerides, and insulin. These are, of course, hard on your brain and your heart. Apparently the red wine suppressed the brain-damaging effects of a high-glycemic meal while boosting neuroprotective antioxidant levels in the blood. So, enjoy a little red wine. But remember, in moderation for your mind.

One study attributed the brain-healthy effects of wine with a meal to the more acidic state that wine creates in the stomach. Wine turns to acetic acid, which is known to delay the quick rise of sugar into the blood and brain after a meal. It is also believed that vinegar and lemon juice, in a salad dressing for instance, can also help improve your digestive system's contribution to a fit and healthy brain.

Snack Attack

Now you have the basics of 20/20 Brain Power meal planning. Of course, sometimes three square meals a day just are not enough. Sometimes you need a snack or two during the day just to keep going.

Most of us have mentally strenuous days, more often than not. Three square meals is typically not enough nourishment for a hungry brain. Of course, your brain is most hungry when it is running at peak torque, such as when you are under pressure, in fear, facing a deadline, or coping with an emotionally wrenching situation. Your brain burns sugar so fast during these times that it often runs out way before your next meal. You know the feeling — I call it the sugar slump.

Brain snacks are simple yet superb ways to keep your brain engine running between meals. They will help keep your brain blood sugar steady and balanced, while supplying your neurotransmitters with their much-needed nutrients. Sometime between breakfast and lunch, when you feel a little energy leaving your brain, do not wait for the crash, have a brain snack.

Mid-Morning Brain Snacks

- 20/20 Brain Baggie: fill a sandwich baggie full of nuts and stuff. Walnuts, peanuts (if you are not allergic), pumpkin seeds, some raisins or craisins (dried cranberries), and an apple. Optionally, you can add dark red, purple, or black grapes. You can prepare your Brain Baggie at home and then snack on it during a break, or throughout the day.
- High-protein, low-carb whey bar
- A Berry Brainy Smoothie (see Recipe Book)

There is no mystery in the English practice of tea at 4:00 in the afternoon. That coincidentally happens to be the same time the brain's blood sugar reserves seem to be at their lowest. Unfortunately, the typical American break generally includes cookies, cakes, or candy — the worst snacks you can give your brain. Sure, they give you a quick lift, but at what cost? Why not try a little tea (green) or coffee, a brisk walk outside, a brainy protein bar or baggie, or a protein drink instead.

I don't like to promote coffee since it has been shown to have some drawbacks. Too much coffee can cause blood sugar ups and downs, possibly dopamine depletion, and an elevation of brain- and heart-damaging homocysteine. However, if used consciously a little coffee can boost brain energy levels. Recently, coffee intake has been correlated with lower incidence of diabetes, Parkinson's and Alzheimer's. Nevertheless, try to keep your coffee consumption below three cups per day.

Afternoon Delights

- Walnuts, peanuts, low-fat mozzarella cheese, apples, peanut butter
- Protein bars (low-carb)
- A brisk walk
- A spot of tea or coffee

The best brainpower teas are black and green tea. There are also teas with ginkgo and ginseng added. Ginkgo, ginseng, and green tea are also available as supplements, which tend to be more potent than the teas.

When Food Is Not Enough

Each of us has our own unique brain biochemistry and it is impacted by our lifestyle choices. Stress, alcohol, junk food, sleep loss, depression, sugar intake, lack of exercise, even anxiety, all influence our need for brain-essential nutrients. That is why we have to eat the right brain foods, in the right way. But even when we do follow a brain-healthy diet as closely as possible, some neuro-nutritional needs are still hard to adequately fulfill. That's why the next chapter is devoted to brain-essential nutritional supplements — insurance for your brain.

10

Neuroceuticals

Supplemental Insurance for Your Brain

"Time bears away all things, even our minds"

Virgil, 70 B.C.

M any of the fruits and vegetables we eat are no longer as nutrient-dense as they were in the past. Chemical fertilizers, pesticides, and fungicides often rob the soil, and the plant, of vital nutrients, thus yielding crops that are lacking the vitamins and minerals they once contained. As a result, many of the basic foods in the American diet are low in certain key brain-vital nutrients. These include vitamins B1, B5, B6, chromium, CoQ10, magnesium, selenium, and zinc. Several of these can be found in natural whole grains, but not even a trace is found in their refined state. Chromium, for example, is normally found in grains. Unfortunately, it gets processed out when the whole grain is reduced to brain-damaging, denatured white flour. Lack of chromium in the diet is a major contributing factor to brain sugar and insulin problems, such as Metabolic Syndrome and diabetes.

Chromium is an important glucose tolerance factor. This means chromium enhances your cells' sugar metabolism and efficiency. As a result, chromium can help normalize insulin levels. Best of all, insulin resistance can be reversed. When you have enough chromium in your diet it takes less sugar to serve your brain cell needs. Brain cells become less sugar addicted and dependent, which makes your little neurons, membranes, and mitochondria very happy, healthy, and functional. If you choose to supplement with chromium, chromium polynicotinate (Chromate) or chromium picolinate seem to be the best forms.

Even when we are eating the highest-quality foods available it can still be almost impossible to derive enough of some nutrients from them. A brain-healthy daily dose of vitamin E, for example, can range from 400 IUs to 1,200 IUs, perhaps even more if you are experiencing serious memory loss. To get 400 IUs on a daily basis from your diet would require you to eat over 100 pounds of meat or poultry liver, or 100 tablespoons of peanut butter, often cited as a good source of vitamin E, as well as a good source of protein, monounsaturated oil, and phoshatidyl choline.

It is also very difficult to get enough vitamin C from our foods. This is especially true if your stress level, or alcohol intake, are high. Unlike most animals, humans cannot synthesize vitamin C. It must be derived from foods and supplements.

Vegetarians are sometimes at risk for low levels of important brain-essential nutrients, such as vitamins B2, B6, and B12, and the minerals selenium and zinc, as well as DHA and other brain-essential fatty acids. It is also difficult for vegetarians to get enough carnitine and carnosine. Carnitine, an amino-acid like nutrient, is important for energy and fat-burning. Carnosine has been heralded as one of the most important antiaging nutrients because of the role it plays in reducing sugar damage to cells. It has also been shown to help relieve cells of heavy-metal toxicity.

Lifestyle factors, such as alcohol, stress, sleep loss, and a poor diet, especially when it consists of too many trans fats and high-glycemic carbohydrates, are known to deplete the body's level of many vital nutrients. This includes many of the brain-essential B vitamins, vitamin C, chromium and magnesium, DHA, and DHEA, which is an important and necessary hormone that declines as we age.

As we age the body's ability to absorb and metabolize the nutrients from our food also declines. Vitamin B12 in particular is difficult for many seniors to absorb. The body's ability to synthesize DHA from many non-fish Omega-3 foods, such as flaxseeds, declines rapidly as we age. Unless we get enough DHA from fish oil daily, our membranes can suffer.

Whether the nutrients are lacking in your diet, or are too quickly used up because of your stress or lifestyle choices, or because you have some existing biochemical imbalance, supplementing with important brain-supportive nutrients can enhance your brain performance and longevity. Should you take supplements to cover the shortages of brain-essential nutrients you may be experiencing? I know I do.

I take vitamins and minerals, amino acids, enzymes, essential fatty acids, and natural herbal supplements, which all help to provide my brain with most of the neuroprotective and performance-boosting antioxidants and cofactors that are known or believed to support healthy brain function. A cofactor is a nutrient that acts as a catalyst for a metabolic process. For example, some of the B vitamins provide important enzymatic reactions that enable the brain to synthesize acetylcholine, dopamine, serotonin, and norepinephrine.

If you have Internet access you can research almost any nutrient you are interested in within a matter of minutes. Don't be afraid to do that. Check everything out for yourself. The following is a list of the supplements I frequently use and that you might want to consider.

Vitamins and Minerals

VITAMIN B COMPLEX: B1 aids mitochondrial ATP energy production. B2 improves DNA synthesis and energy. B3 supports ATP energy and ACh synthesis. B5 is an ACh cofactor and works synergistically with B1 and B3 to make ATP in the mitochondria. B6 supports serotonin and norepinephrine production, RNA and DNA. B9 (folic acid) reduces homocysteine and aids RNA/DNA synthesis. B12 helps regulate homocysteine and repair neurological damage. Suggested dosage is one to two B50 complexes over the day.

VITAMIN E: Protects membranes and capillaries from lipid oxidation. Best for your brain are the tocotrienols, as well as gamma tocopherol. (Note: In nature vitamin E exists as four isomers (alpha, beta, gamma, and delta) of tocopherol and four of tocotrienol). Vitamin E is now available at many health food stores as mixed tocopherols and tocotrienols, or a mixed tocopherol blend labeled "High in

Gamma-E." The most common form of vitamin E, dl-alpha-tocopherol, is a synthetic version that has mixed clinical results. I suggest taking a 400 IU capsule of mixed tocopherols with gamma, or a mixture of all tocopherols and tocotrienols with or right after two or three meals. Note: Vitamin E is best taken with vitamin C.

VITAMIN C: Protects brain cells and capillaries from free radicals and inflammation, and aids in the formation of several neurotransmitters. Vitamin C is best when taken in mineral ascorbate form, as Ester-C™, or as the fat-soluble ascorbyl palmitate. Suggested dosage is 500 to 1,000 mg. of mineral ascorbates (such as calcium ascorbate, or mixed mineral ascorbates), or the same of Ester-C™, and 500 mg. ascorbyl palmitate (a fat-soluble form of vitamin C) per meal.

MINERALS: The most absorbable forms are citrate, glycinate, malate, orotate, and ascorbate. Chromium (best as polynicotinate) helps blood sugar balance. Magnesium protects membranes and mitochondria, improves neural impulse conduction (speed), and is involved in many enzymatic reactions. It also helps blood sugar and has been shown to lower hypertension. Potassium helps balance sodium and provides energy for brain cells. Selenium works synergistically with other brain antioxidants, such as vitamin E and CoQ10, and is a key brain antioxidant that is often low in the diet. It can also play an anti-inflammatory role. Zinc is a catalyst in many important reactions and is highly concentrated in the hippocampus, the learning and memory center of the brain. Iron is important but its necessity is highly individualized. Women and children tend toward deficiency. Men need to be careful of iron overload. Suggested daily dosages: Chromium polynicotinate, 200 to 600 mcg.; Magnesium (citrate or aspartate or orotate), 400-800 mg.; Potassium (citrate or aspartate or orotate), 100 – 500 mg.; Selenium (as selenomethionine), 100-300 mcg.; Zinc, 15-30 mg. Take any of these mineral supplements with or between meals.

Fats and Lipids, Amino Acids, and Enzymes

FISH OIL CAPSULES: DHA is the mainstay of brain cell membranes; it improves transmembrane signaling and cellular function; it helps regulate the effects of stress, and high glucose and insulin. It is as vital to healthy brain cells as calcium is to bones. It helps increase natural brain production of dopamine and serotonin. In supplements look for labels that say molecularly distilled. This means it is essentially pharmaceutical-grade in quality, and especially purity. Nondistilled oils run the risk of contamination, such as from mercury. Suggested daily DHA dosages: 500 to 1,500 mg. Take with meals and vitamin E.

PHOSPHATIDYL CHOLINE (PC) is a superior form of choline. Choline is endorsed by the U.S. government as a vital nutrient. PC is derived from lecithin (soybeans and eggs); is an integral part of brain cell membrane; main fuel (precursor) for synthesis of acetylcholine, the brain processing speed neurotransmitter. Lecithin and PC also contain inositol, another great brain and membrane nutrient. When taken with meals they can help keep cholesterol levels in check, which of course is also good for the brain. Note: Standard lecithin is only 10 to 20 percent PC. Therefore, look for Triple Lecithin, Super Lecithin, or PC. Better yet, get PC powder (30 to 50 percent PC) and use it in smoothies (1 TBS), or sprinkle on oatmeal or cereal.

PHOSPHATIDYL SERINE (PS) is also derived from lecithin (soybeans and eggs) and is an integral part of the brain cell membrane. PS is the only brain-essential nutrient that has U. S. government approval for brain claims. PS has been shown to improve memory. It also helps reduce abnormal cortisol levels, and is a vital component of healthy cell membranes. Suggested dosage is 100 to 300 mg. a day, preferably with food.

ALPHA LIPOIC ACID (ALA) is a powerful antioxidant and neuro-protector. ALA revitalizes the other neuroprotective agents, such as vitamins E and C and CoQ10. It increases brain levels of glutathione, an important antioxidant brain protector and immune system booster. ALA also improves blood sugar balance, lowers insulin resistance, and reduces the glycation of proteins, or AGE plaque formation. It has been shown to improve memory. ALA, when combined with acetyl-L-carnitine has shown remarkable and well documented synergistic effects in slowing down brain aging at the mitochondrial level.

CARNITINE is a key to energy metabolism in the mitochondria; may also improve ACh function, offer neuroprotection, and possibly stimulate neurogenesis. Carnitine is also used in weight loss, endurance-enhancing, and muscle-building formulas. It is available from meat but in limited amounts. It is best supplemented. It is also depleted by stress and alcohol. Note: The acetylated form, acetyl-L-carnitine, is believed to be more brain active than carnitine. Suggested dosage is 500 to 1500 mg. a day, especially if you are physically active.

N-ACETYL-CYSTEINE (NAC) is an amino acid with powerful antioxidant, neuroprotective properties. NAC is a precursor of glutathione, one of the most powerful endogenous immune enhancers. NAC and glutathione fight brain inflammation as well as free radicals. NAC also chelates heavy metals, such as lead and mercury, lightening their toxic load on the brain. Some studies suggest that combining NAC with other antioxidants, such as Curcumin and certain B vitamins, can significantly reduce the risk for developing Alzheimer's later in life. Suggested dosage is 250 to 500 mg. a day.

COQ10 is an important antioxidant; necessary for mitochondrial ATP energy production; protects the mitochondria; works synergistically with vitamin E and selenium. Suggested dosage is 100 to 300 mg. a day in soft gel form.

Plants and Herbs

CURCUMIN (Curc): The active polyphenol compound in the bright yellowish-orange spice turmeric, Curc is a powerful COX-2 inhibitor. It also reduces brain inflammation via other pathways such as LOX-5 as well as highly damaging NOS- (nitric oxide-) based peroxynitrites. Curc is also a powerful antioxidant and neuroprotective agent. Perhaps most remarkably, it has demonstrated the ability to prevent the formation of the telltale Alzheimer's plaques known as beta amyloid, or Abeta. In fact, studies even revealed that Curc can reduce the existing plaque burden of Abeta. Suggested dosage is 250 to 500 mg. a day.

GINKGO BILOBA: Although much of the medical community has not yet endorsed ginkgo for memory enhancement in Mild Cognitive Impairment or Alzheimer's disease, few would deny that it has very powerful neuroprotective effects. Ginkgo increases blood flow to the brain; improves brain glucose metabolism and efficiency, synthesis of neurotransmitters and energy production of mitochondria; reduces platelet clumping (sticky blood) and inflammation; and protects the brain when there is a loss of oxygen. Ginkgo has been shown to improve memory, processing speed, and attention in clinical trials. Look for standardized 24 or 27 percent flavonglycosides. I believe when it comes to protecting your memory, Gingko is truly a brainsaving gift from nature. Suggested dosage is 60 to 120 mg. a day.

GINSENG: Well known for all its purported powers to boost sexual energy and stamina. However, the real treasure of ginseng could be that certain forms may help rejuvenate the brain. Panax Ginseng supports the ACh system, protects the hippocampal (L&M) neurons, and may sensitize the extremely important hypothalamus, pituitary, and adrenal cells (the HPA axis), which is important in the regulation of cortisol. For its anti-stress benefits Ginseng is known as an adaptogenic herb. It helps to normalize HPA function and reduce the brain-damaging effects of cortisol. Ginseng alone, or in combination with ginkgo has been clinically shown to improve brain speed and memory in brain healthy individuals. Suggested dosage is two to three capsules, with a minimum of 30 percent ginsenosides, the active ingredient.

GREEN TEA: An important source of powerful neuroprotective agents, such as the polyphenol, epigallocatechin gallate (EGCG), and theanine, an alertness promoter, as well as neuroprotective agent. Green tea also helps with blood sugar regulation, and improves cerebral vascular health. Although drinking several cups of green tea a day is beneficial, it was recently shown that taking two to three capsules of green tea extract results in greater absorption of the active ingredients.

Neuro Hormones

DHEA: A hormone naturally manufactured by the adrenals and parts of the brain. Endogenous levels decline sharply after age 30. Hundreds of studies have shown that DHEA works on multiple levels to improve memory; reduce the brain cell-destroying effects of stress (cortisol); improve insulin sensitivity and glucose tolerance; reduce depression and raise energy levels; and, slow down the effects of aging. Another form, 7-Keto DHEA is preferred by many scientists. I suggest 25 to 50 mg. a day. However, many believe it is important to first test your DHEA blood or saliva levels so that you don't raise your DHEA levels too high. It is important to seek the guidance of a health care practitioner when it comes to hormones.

Melatonin (MEL): A hormone naturally manufactured by the pineal gland. Long heralded as a supplement to enhance sleep, MEL has recently been shown to exert a number of powerful, brain specific anti-oxidant and anti-inflammatory effects. MEL has been clinically shown to: protect against neuro-toxic after effects of stroke, to improve memory, and to act as an anti-depressant. Most importantly, it has recently been shown to reduce the beta amyloid plaques associated with Alzheimer's.

Supplementing Specifically For Brain Speed

Your brain's performance and longevity are based on its blood flow, its supply of neurotransmitters, the health of its membranes and mitochondria, and its synapses and their collective ability to rapidly communicate with other cells throughout your brain. As you have learned, the primary neurotransmitters involved in memory and cognition are acetylcholine (ACh), glutamate, serotonin, dopamine, and norepinephrine. Of these, acetylcholine, glutamate, norepinephrine, and dopamine excite, or activate, neuronal processes and are therefore called excitatory neurotransmitters. Serotonin is an inhibitory neurotransmitter, which acts to calm the brain.

Acetylcholine (ACh) is your brain speed molecule, at least for perception, learning, attention, thinking, and working memory. Synthesized by your brain cells from choline, acetylcholine helps you pay attention and improves the formation of short-term memories. Choline is an essential dietary nutrient. It is responsible for a broad range of functions from the creation of acetylcholine to speedy transmembrane and neuron-to-neuron signal transmission. The structure and function of brain cell membranes and the transport and metabolism of cholesterol are all dependent on sufficient choline. In pregnant women, low prenatal and breast-milk levels of choline result in lower IQs and more cognitive impairment in children, plus accelerated cognitive decline as they are growing up. Choline levels in the brain have been correlated with IQ. Later in life, deficits of choline and acetylcholine prestage serious memory loss and Alzheimer's.

Although choline is naturally manufactured by the liver, its primary source is from your diet. The principal dietary sources of choline are eggs, fish and soy products, such as lecithin — the source of phosphatidyl choline (PC). PC is also found in certain nuts, such as peanuts and peanut butter, and Krill (small, shrimp-like crustaceans). Choline is found to a much lesser degree in dark leafy greens.

As we age, reduced cerebral vascular blood flow and naturally lower choline levels result in less acetylcholine for our hungry neurons. Lower acetylcholine levels results in slower thinking, compromised concentration and attention span, and reduced ability to learn and remember. Alzheimer's disease and mild cognitive impairment (MCI) are characterized by a reduction in the brain's synthesis and utilization of ACh.

As we get older there is also an increase in our brain's production of the enzyme acetylcholinesterase (AChE). AChE metabolizes (eats up) acetylcholine before it can be adequately used by our worn and weary neurons. If that isn't bad enough, as we age the accumulated effects of poor nutrition, bad brain fats, alcohol, stress and sugar, all gang up on our brain and impair its ability to make and use acetylcholine. Even worse, the reduced availability of choline in the blood causes our choline-hungry neurons to literally cannibalize available choline molecules from the cell membranes. This further impairs the speed and efficiency of neurotransmission by compromising membrane structure and function. All of these factors combine to slow down brain speed and mental acuity, and fuzz up intracranial communications.

Measurable Speed

The true test of any nutrient's power to improve cognitive performance is its ability to increase the brain's speed and efficiency in processing information. Fortunately, brain speed can now be measured by various computer programs and Internet-based tests. The millisecond measurement of brain speed is the secret to determining how quickly foods, supplements, diets, exercise (mental or physical), or any combination of the above can truly improve memory, attention, mental quickness, and brain speed. In fact, hundreds of FDA-approved clinical trials have used mental reaction speed tests to objectively assess the subtle brain-boosting effects of many pharmaceutical drugs and natural brain supplements.

To improve your brain's processing speed and efficiency you can increase your intake of choline foods. You can also take certain supplements to improve acetylcholine synthesis and utilization, as well as improve membrane and mitochondrial function. You can combine these with other supplements proven to enhance brain metabolism and energy and increase brain blood flow. This improves your brain's supply and utilization of vital nutrients, such as oxygen, glucose, and choline.

You can use certain safe and natural supplements to enhance blood flow to your brain, increase your brain's metabolism, and improve membrane function and mitochondria energy (ATP) production. You can also use supplements to improve your brain's utilization of oxygen and glucose, and the efficient synthesis and utilization of acetylcholine. When your brain is receiving everything it needs to function optimally you can noticeably increase your brain's processing speed, improve your memory and concentration, and your executive thinking, problem solving, and decision-making performance. Here are three powerful, natural supplements that can be combined to help you achieve 20/20 Brain Power, fast.

Note: Since the first publishing of this book the following brain nutrients have been clinically shown to improve memory, mental energy, clarity and even IQ. For more information on this unique proprietary formula called ProceraAVH™ see Appendix I, Breakthrough Clinical Discovery. When you combine acetyl-L-carnitine, vinpocetine and Huperzine A in specific amounts and ratios (my ProceraAVH formula as defined in my Patent Application), there appears to be a synergistic effect that is not obvious from the many years of research and clinical use with these individual ingredients. This points out the unique synergy that certain combinations of natural ingredients can have. Also go to www.BrainResearchLabs.com.

HUPERZINE A (HupA) is derived from Chinese Club Moss (Huperia serrata). It is a natural acetylcholinesterase (AChE) inhibitor. Remember, AChE is the enzyme that destroys ACh in the synapse before it is effectively used. That means that HupA helps keep your acetylcholine levels up, so your synapses fire fast and efficiently. HupA has been shown to improve memory, protect brain cells both from free radical and glutamate "excitotoxicity," a highly damaging condition found in accelerated brain aging and Alzheimer's. HupA also stimulates the acetylcholine receptors, making them more sensitive to existing levels of ACh. HupA may also act as a brain metabolic enhancer. Recommended dose is 100 to 150 mcg. per day.

VINPOCETINE (VIN) is a natural extract of the beautiful periwinkle flower. It increases cerebral vascular blood flow, thus enhancing the flow of nutrients, oxygen, glucose, and choline to the brain. VIN has been shown to improve memory and brain processing speed. It also increases brain glucose metabolism and increases the availability of ATP, which improves brain energy. It is also a powerful neuroprotective agent that has been shown to protect brain cells after the sudden loss of oxygen. The recommended dose is 5 to 15 mg. per day. Note: for optimal absorption VIN must be taken with food in stomach.

ACETYL-L-CARNITINE (ALC) is perhaps the one true miracle molecule, especially for your brain (and heart). ALC is naturally found in the brain and body. Its main dietary source is red meat. ALC has multiple roles in the protection, preservation, and performance of your brain cells. It increases brain blood flow, as well as the production and utilization of ACh. It improves the energy output of your mighty mitochondria, helps stabilize the membrane, and protects both from free radical damage. ALC increases acetylcholine levels in the brain. It has been shown to protect the brain even after a head injury or stroke, and helps accelerate the healing of damaged neurons. It is believed to help remove a serious brain-damaging plaque, a dark pigment called lipofuscin. ALC also increases levels of glutathione, perhaps the brain's most powerful antioxidant. ALC has also been shown to increase levels of nerve growth factor, thus stimulating neurogenesis. In fact, ALC appears to rejuvenate the brain and significantly slow brain aging. It helps protect the brain from excess alcohol, or its more brain-harmful byproduct, acetylaldehyde. It also helps neutralize the harmful free radicals normally generated by the cellular process of ATP energy generation. Dozens of studies have demonstrated ALC's powerful effect on improving attention, reducing depression, and boosting memory, processing speed and cognitive function, in both normal and impaired individuals. Recommended daily dose is 500 to 1,500 mg. to be taken with or right after a meal, and best when divided between two or three meals.

These wonderful brain nutrients can be combined in a certain ratio to render an incredibly powerful synergistic effect significantly improving mental energy, clarity, and actual performance. When you combine acetyl-L-carnitine, vinpocetine and Huperzine A they enhance each other's positive brainpower effects.

Table 10.1 contains a rating system that I developed regarding the most popular and widely recognized brain nutrients. The nutrients are listed in the far left column and potential benefits are listed across the top. Optimally you want a nutrient to have benefits in as many columns as possible.

Sleep On It

Even when it seems your body has gotten a good night's sleep it does not necessarily mean that your brain has. Haven't you ever had one of those mornings when you awaken feeling good physically, but a little dull mentally?

When you want to relieve your body of stress you sleep. Unfortunately, most sleep, especially as we age, does not adequately discharge deep-seated neural stress, the kind that initially limits our mental performance and brain speed, and ultimately damages our brain cells.

You can help your sleep with: a light load of carbs, such as half a banana just before bed. A sublingual dose of melatonin, or an herbal tea or a pill with valerian may also help. Also try 100-300 mg of L-Theanine (a generally available nutraceutical derived from green tea), 100-200 mg of 5-HTP (5-Hydroxytrypto-phan, a precursor to serotonin) one hour before going to bed and/or 2-3 grams of Glycine. Any one or more of these can help you shuffle off to slumberland.

While those sleep aids are all very helpful, if you really want to de-stress your mind and relieve your body of stress you will want to learn about Neural Need Number Three – neural rest and relaxation. In the next chapter I am going to teach you about the importance of the Alpha Brain Break, a practical and effective technique for achieving complete brain stress reduction.

Major Effects of Leading Brain Nutrients

BRAIN NUTRIENT	MAJOR EFFECT							
	Increases Brain Speed			Neuroprotective		Other Effects		
	Enhances Acetyl-choline	Improves Oxygen &/or Glucose Utilization	Enhances Brain Metabolism	Anti-Oxidant	Anti-Inflammatory	Improves Memory	Improves Focus	Improves Quality of Sleep
ALC	●	●	○	●		●	●	○
Vinpocetine	○	●	●	●		●	○	
Huperzine A	●		○	●		○	○	
DHEA		●	○	○	○	○	○	
Fish Oil				○	●	●	○	○
Phosphatidyl Choline	○			○		○	○	
Ginkgo	○	○		●		○		
Ginseng		●		○		●		
Phosphatidyl Serine	○			○		○		
Alpha Lipoic Acid		●	○	●		○		
Green Tea		○	○	●				
Vitamin E		○		●	○			
Curcumin				●	●	○		
N-Acetyl-Cysteine				●	○			
Vitamin Bs (1,2,3,5,6,12 & folate)	○	○		●			○	○
Vitamin C				○	○			
Minerals (Cr, Mg, Se, Zn)		●		○	○			
Theanine				○			○	○
Melatonin	○			●	●			●
5-HTP						○		●

● **Primary Effect**
○ **Secondary Effect**

Table 10.1

11

The Alpha Brain Break

The Art and Science of Brain Rest and Relaxation

*"An Alpha Brain Break is the quickest way to
clear your mind and recharge your brain".*

Joshua Reynolds

Your brain can do only so much hard work before it gets tired and starts losing efficiency. When your brain is fatigued, no matter what you are doing, you are not going to be doing it as well as you would if your brain were clear, sharp, and relaxed. A fatigued brain is foggy, forgetful, confused, and spaced-out. When your brain is overwrought, overtired, or burned out, you feel drained, irritable, and inefficient. You no longer have the brain energy you need to stay sharp, alert, and active. But, as you already know, your mind has no problem overworking your brain. And, since your brain is a very stoic organ, it tries to keep functioning, no matter what. After all, when your brain stops working so do you. So what is a brain to do? Get a little "R&R"… that's what.

In the same way that time-out can be a lifesaver for a child that is reeling from too much stimulation, an Alpha Brain Break is restorative and regenerative to your very deserving brain. But, isn't that what sleeping is all about — rest and recuperation? Not for your brain. Remember, your brain continues to work, even while you are asleep. An Alpha Brain Break is something you do while you are awake. It requires only your conscious choice.

Stress is death to your brain cells. Neuro-relaxation begins with stress management and ends with a brain break – a temporary, but complete cessation of automatic and reactionary thinking that can restore your mind's full capacity and natural brilliance in just five to 10 minutes. Stress management is critically important to your brain. In this chapter I am gong to give you the techniques you need to meet your brain's third essential need – stress release and relaxation.

Static in Your Attic

Your brain's processing speed is an important indicator of your brainpower. However, mental clarity depends on processing efficiency. In a computer, when there are too many programs running and it starts acting quirky, it can be a sign that the computer processor's efficiency is significantly compromised. In your brain, when one processing center receives garbled input from another, it is generally a sign that your brain's processing efficiency is compromised. Brain processing efficiency is primarily a function of the level of noise in your neural network.

Let's take a look at some of the basics of electronics for a moment. Every electronic circuit has some noise in it. When you are listening to the radio in your car and you drive out of range of the radio station you are tuned in to you get static, or noise. Or, if you happen to be talking on your cell phone and you drive into a signal drop-off zone, what do you hear? Static. The louder and more persistent the static, the more garbled the voice on the other end. You can't hear what is being said. The information can't get through. Noise corrupts information. The noise in your brain manifests as brain fuzz, mental fog, and forgetfulness. Cognitive scientists call it neural noise. I call it static in your attic.

In the same way that static or noise can ruin your stereo's reproduction of a great symphony, brain noise can distort the clarity of your perceptions, thoughts, choices, and actions. The more neural noise you have, the more muddled and distorted your incoming signals. It really is a case of garbled in, garbled out. The higher the noise level, the more pervasive the static, the less consistently, or efficiently your brain can accurately process (read: file and retrieve) information.

So where does all this static come from? Unfortunately, it has many causes. It increases with age, mental fatigue, and physical exhaustion. Many medications can cause neural noise, as can a poor night's sleep, junk food, lack of exercise, and especially a hangover. However, for the most part neural noise comes from your chattering mind. Mental chatter clutters up your mind. Messages become distorted, errors in calculation more frequent. This can lead to mistakes on the job, or errors in judgment behind the wheel. A noisy, chattering mind can undermine your ability to make a decision, and lock you in a prison of mental confusion and chaos. It distracts you, making concentration almost impossible. All this neural noise affects your mind's creativity, attention span, ability to observe and learn, ability to properly file away new information in your brain, and quickly retrieve it. It diminishes your ability to think fast and act smart. Neural noise decreases your learning efficiency. Perhaps that is why everyone whispers in a library.

But wait a minute, it's true that some days your mind is all mush and fuzz, but other days it is very clear and focused. Maybe that means that neural noise is something changeable. It is indeed. You can quiet your busy mind, clear your head, amplify subtle intuitive signals from within, and boost your mental efficiency. But first…

Chattering Minds Must Go

Of all the desirable mental skills and capacities — memory, thinking speed, and alertness — nothing is more beneficial than having all your awareness in the present moment. Being totally in the moment creates an enormous energy that produces almost supernatural clarity, intuition, and insight. When you are in the moment, the zone, you discover new and consistent powers of mind inaccessible to you when in your normal state of fragmented consciousness.

Normal consciousness for most of us originates from not one, but at least two points of reference. A tiny bit of awareness is in the moment, and the rest is running around with our chattering, wandering mind. Mind is off in the future, back in the past, immersed in superficial thought, or lost in emotional indulgence. For example, how often have you been engaged in a conversation with someone and noticed that you (and maybe even they) are not truly present, that your mind is wandering, or is preoccupied with thoughts of its own? In fact, for you the real conversation is taking place between the voices in your own head. This actually robs you of all of the rewards you might derive from the conversation with the other person because you are not truly present.

An overly chatty or worried mind creates a tense, noisy brain. A tense, noisy brain generates beta waves.

Brain Waves 101

Now, not all beta waves are bad. Beta waves are close to the highest range of brainwave frequencies as captured by an electroencephalogram (EEG). On an oscilloscope beta waves look very noisy and scattered, just like the focus and thinking they often reflect.

Alpha waves, on the other hand, are slower and much more organized, coherent, with the mind more in focus. Alpha lies in the eight to 12 cycles per second range, between beta and theta. The alphatized brain can generate a whopping 10 times more voltage (electricity) than a betafied brain. Lab studies have shown that mental processing speed is much quicker when the brain is in alpha. And, the effect seems to last long after the brain has had even a brief respite in the alpha zone. It is no wonder that many great alphas are also great athletes, leaders, and lovers. Everyone is attracted to those alpha personalities!

A calm and relaxed brain generates abundant alpha waves. Alpha waves promote clear, sharp, and focused thinking. A mind fully present in the moment is an alpha mind. Listening to your favorite relaxing music can put your brain into alpha. So can an Alpha Brain Break.

Understand that you normally experience alpha zone — that relaxed yet totally aware state of mind — at least two times a day, once briefly before falling asleep and again when you first wake up. The alpha zone is that deliciously peaceful, albeit fleeting, space you experience just as you are beginning to doze off and as you begin waking up.

Perhaps no single mental quality guarantees success at all levels, personal and professional, more than being fully and consistently present. Thomas Edison had a highly inventive, productive, and active mind. It is said that every three hours or so he gave his overworked brain a break, or catnap to re-energize his mind and body.

Edison's technique was to sit in a chair, close his eyes, and let himself fall asleep... almost. What he intuitively knew was that the most productive brain discharge and recharge takes place in the twilight, or alpha zone, right at the border between wakefulness and sleep.

It has been proven that the brain discharges significantly more accumulated stress in this alpha zone than during sleep. Many creative minds — Einstein, Mozart, Jonas Salk, Buckminster Fuller, Aldous Huxley, John F. Kennedy, and others all described similar techniques they used to relax their brains, clear their heads, and recharge their neurons. For me, when I enter this wonderful place... I enter the deepest sources of my creativity. I frequently use this space to gain fresh insight into a problem I am trying to solve or even an opportunity that is being presented to me. When your mind is quiet it is open to more information from outer and inner sources. You become much more sensitive to subtle signals from within. And, these can be very important to hear.

After a short five- or 10-minute Alpha Brain Break your brain will be highly energized, fuzz free, and very focused — ready for steady, sustainable performance. You will know what it means when people say they have been in the alpha zone. Once you master the art of the Alpha Brain Break you will find that thinking takes on a whole new nature.

Ordinary thinking is typically automatic and reactive, sometimes even forced. After an Alpha Brain Break, thinking becomes rich, innovative, and easy. Insights and intuitions well up effortlessly from the fertile subterrains of your brain.

Give Your Brain a Break Today

Typically when we think about a break, we think grab a snack, smoke a "choke" (cigarette), chug down a cup of "Joe" or two, share a little gossip over the watercooler, maybe even stare out the window and worry about our problems. However, none of these choices gives your poor brain a break. In fact, they all do just the opposite. Your brain has to keep plugging along, thinking and choosing, analyzing and reacting. What you are going to learn now is how to truly give your brain the break it deserves.

Right before you wake up in the morning you are in your basal, or lowest metabolic state. After you wake up you move into an active-metabolic state. When you are very active or slightly stressed you rev up into a hyper-metabolic state where your heart rate, cortisol and blood pressure levels rise. Unfortunately, none of these states helps you discharge stress. During sleep you are in a slightly reduced basal-metabolic state where surface tensions in your brain cells, and deeper tension in your muscle cells, get released. But, very little deep-seated brain stress gets discharged, especially as your brain ages.

When you are in a hypo-metabolic state your metabolism slows down significantly more than during sleep. This allows your deepest layers of stress, especially neural stress… to release more efficiently. How does an Alpha Brain Break get you into a hypo-metabolic state? Through the Alpha Mind. It has been shown that when in the alpha state one's metabolism can slow down even more than during sleep. This significantly reduced metabolic state is called a hypo-metabolic state. The hypo-metabolic state achieved during a five- to 10-minute Alpha Brain Break is so physiologically powerful that your stress hormone (cortisol) levels, free radicals, and blood pressure can all drop dramatically. See Table 11.1

Positive Effects of an Alpha Brain Break on the Brain and Body	
INCREASES	DECREASES
Glucose and oxygen utilization	Cortisol—adrenaline, norepinephrine
Brain healthy hormones such as DHEA	Insulin resistance
Immune system	Blood sugar levels
Brain-body health and fitness	Oxidative stress and free radicals
Brain speed and focus	Inflammation
Mental clarity	Blood pressure

Table 11.1

As I indicated earlier, the hypo-metabolic state is that deliciously refreshing headspace you are in so briefly right before you fall asleep, and right after you wake up. Unfortunately, it lasts only a few moments. That is, unless you learn how to extend and prolong it.

The Name Game

Resonance is a principle of physics. Electronic circuits or systems can have certain resonant frequencies wherein their operational efficiency, clarity, and power are all optimal. When a system is out of resonance, or tune, its efficiency is highly compromised. For example, when the spark plugs in a high-performance engine are firing out of timing the engine's performance sputters and suffers.

Every electronic circuit, including your brain and nervous system, has a resonant frequency at which it operates in optimal harmony and performance. A vibrationally tuned brain is experienced as crystal clarity, heightened mental acuity, and decisive mental quickness.

Physics lesson number two — you can bring about resonance in a system by introducing a very specific sound vibration. This is what is happening when a great opera singer's vibrato vibrates a crystalline windowpane or wineglass to shatter its crystalline matrix.

Electronic circuitry aside, your brain is a clump of highly organized cells and molecules. Like most molecules it can be influenced by sound. And, although crystal glass requires an audible sound to resonate its molecules, your brain cells can respond to silent words and sounds, such as your brain name.

Scientists using sophisticated electroencephalogram (EEG) machines to measure brain waves have shown that certain brain names, when quietly recited in the mind, have tremendous power to induce resonance in your nervous system, cohere neural noise, synchronize the brain waves and even hemispheres, reconnect disparate parts of the brain, and produce a deep state of alpha consciousness.

As this process of resonance spreads across the brain, enlisting more and more cells into a harmonious cacophony of synchronous brainwaves, a new state of consciousness emerges. You see, although your brain has merely slowed down to very low alpha frequencies, which is around eight cycles per second, your mind has also slowed down, stopped its distracting chatter, and entered the magnificent moment. The brain has silently slipped into the alpha zone. Quite content, you experience a wondrous wave of peacefulness, clarity, and creativity, without thought, or at least the automatic thinking you are used to. You and your brain feel connected to your mind, body, and soul, and to the world at large.

The Benefits of Alpha Brain Breaks

- Increase brain speed
- Enhance memory and concentration
- Boost IQ (shown in schoolchildren doing a brain break technique)
- Heighten (awaken) creativity, intuition, and insight
- Dramatically reduce stress and dangerous cortisol levels
- Reduce harmful levels of serum lactate, epinephrine (adrenaline), norepinephrine (noradrenaline) and blood sugar
- Lower free radicals and lipid peroxides (membrane-damaging)
- Reduce glucose and insulin levels
- Lower blood pressure and heart rate
- Promote peace and clarity of mind
- Elevate mood
- Eliminate fatigue
- Relieve depression
- Lessen anxiety
- Improve overall health (and probably longevity)

Now here is the technique:

You can't do an Alpha Brain Break without a Brain Name. Choosing it can take a few minutes so plan to give this exercise your full attention, with as few distractions as possible. There are three names to choose from: Ahh eemmm, Sheee ohm, and Neeerrr inggg. One is sure to be just right for you.

First, sit comfortably, in your bed, in a chair, or on a couch. Make sure you are absolutely comfy, but not lying down. Close your eyes, and begin to relax. Begin breathing more deeply. Breathe deeper and deeper, listening to each breath – in and out. Do this for a minute or so, and then...

Silently say the following sound – Ahh eeemmm... Ahh eeemmm... Ahh eeemmm... Imagine it as one word on a continuous tape loop. As you continue repeating the sound to yourself, vary the speed of repetition. Try slower, then faster, then slower again, and so on until you find a rhythm that feels comfortable and almost effortless for you. Feel how it resonates with your brain.

Continue reciting the sound silently until it feels like you can hear it ringing in your head. Don't get discouraged if you don't hear it right away. If a thought wanders into your mind and distracts you, simply observe it, don't engage it or let it trigger a string of random chatter. Just stay focused on your word, or sound. Relax and let go. Plunge fully into moment. Don't doze off. Sit upright, especially if you are still in bed.

Now try the next Brain Name – Sheee ohm… Sheee ohm… Sheee ohm … and continue the same process as above for two to three minutes. Finally, try the sound Neeerrr inggg… Neeerrr inggg… Neeerrr inggg… and give it your full attention for the next two or three minutes.

After you have tried all three Brain Names choose ONE. You can do it now, or you can allow yourself to feel them out over the course of a day. You may even begin to hear your brain name pop into your mind much like a phrase or tune from one of your favorite songs. Choose the name you feel the most resonance with, the one that feels most comfortable to your brain. Once you choose your Brain Name, commit to using it every day, at least during your 20-Day Brain Power Program.

Once you have committed to your brain name you can take your first Alpha Brain Break. You can do it mid- to late afternoon, when your energy is sagging, or in the morning right after you awake, whenever you feel you need it.

An Alpha Brain Break can last from five to 15 minutes. Some days your brain will respond faster than others. Some days it will need more time, some days a little less. In truth, if your practice establishes a good, conditioned response — recite name, unwind and de-stress brain — it can take as little five minutes in the alpha state to get a full neural discharge and recharge.

Begin your brain break by silently saying your Brain Name. As you continue repeating your brain name silently in your mind, vary its speed of repetition. Slower, then faster, then slower again, and so on, until you find a rhythm that feels comfortable, almost effortless. Feel how the sound of your brain name resonates with your mind. Continue reciting the sound silently in your mind until it feels like you can hear it ringing or singing in your head. Don't get discouraged if you don't hear it right away. Keep listening for, or to it, attentively for the next two or three minutes. Relax and totally let go. Allow yourself to plunge fully into the moment. Don't fall asleep. Stay awake for your entire Alpha Brain Break.

Heady Intruders

One of the first things you will notice is the intrusion of thoughts, or a stream of mental chatter. All you do is notice it, let the thoughts be, don't engage and chase them with conscious afterthoughts. Watch them and the thinking process subside. Go back to your brain name. Reciting your name or listening to its sound will progressively hold more and more of your intrusive thoughts at bay.

How will you know when you are in the alpha zone? You will know because you will feel like you are firmly seated and relaxed in a very still, clear, and expansive inner space. Afterwards your brain will feel reenergized if not rejuvenated. You will feel refreshed and ready to get up and get going.

Starting Your Own Journey to 20/20 Brain Power

Now that you have read this book, you might be experiencing a little brain stress and duress from trying to absorb it all. I know I have given your brain an incredible amount of information to process. Remember, challenging your mind to learn something new is one of the best ways to build new brain cells and keep your brain young and sharp. Now you are about to pull it all together and put it into practice.

Why not give your brain a much needed makeover and take the next 20 days, if not the rest of your life to address and satisfy your brain's three essential needs? Don't you owe it to your "poor", over worked and under nurtured noggin?

Putting your brain through at least 20 days of brain healthy nutrition, exercise and stress relief can and will save your brain, and keep it sharp for many years to come. Plus, your efforts will reward you with a lifetime guarantee of optimal brain health and longevity, and peak mental performance – on demand. What have you got to lose? Nothing. And, you have everything to gain.

May your brain powers and wisdom soar so you can better serve your self and others!

Until one is committed,
There is hesitancy,
The chance to draw back,
Always ineffectiveness.

Concerning all acts of initiative (and creation),
There is one elemental truth,
The ignorance of which kills countless ideas and splendid plans:
That the moment one definitely commits oneself,
Then providence moves too.

All sorts of things occur to help one
That would never otherwise have occurred.
A whole stream of events
Issues from the decision,
Raising in one's favor,
All manner of unforeseen incidents and meetings and material assistance,
Which no man could have dreamed would have come his way.

Whatever you can do or dream you can
Begin it
Boldness has genius, magic and power in it
Begin it now

Goethe

Appendix I

Breakthrough Clinical Discovery

In Chapter 10 I talked about the wonderful brain boosting effects of three natural supplements, Acetyl-l-carnitine, Vinpocetine and Huperzine A. Although these ingredients have each been studied and found safe and effective in over 50 years of cumulative research and clinical use, never before have just these three powerful brain nutrients been combined and subjected to an FDA-type, double blind, randomized and placebo controlled clinical trial with a significant number of people.

In early November, 2007 Dr. Con Stough, head of the world famous Brain Sciences Institute at the prestigious Swinburne University in Australia, presented the findings of a year long study to an international group of medical news reporters and research scientists at the exclusive World Nutra conference in Reno, NV.

Dr. Stough's study enrolled over 100 normal, mentally healthy people ages 21-66. Approximately half were randomly placed in a group who received the three ingredients, Acetyl-l-carnitine, Vinpocetine and Huperzine A in a specific ratio and amount comprising my Formula, ProceraAVH. The balance of the group received a placebo, or inactive pill. Neither the university researchers or the study participants knew whether they were on ProceraAVH or the placebo.

Prior to starting and finishing the 30 day study, all participants took a 4 hour battery of standardized cognitive and mood tests, including a well known Wechlser IQ test called Ravens Progressive Matrices.

Dr. Stough's presentation to an international group of medical press reporters and nutritional science researchers created quite a buzz. From a historical review of the ingredient list many in the audience already new that one or more of the three ingredients, at a high enough dosage level can improve brain speed, memory and attention (or, focus and concentration). However, no one, including me, the inventor of ProceraAVH was expecting what the professor revealed to a very quiet and curious audience.

Participants on ProceraAVH but not on the placebo showed significant improvements in both short term learning and recall, and long term memory, especially in the speed of recall. In fact, the ProceraAVH group, with an average age 48, experienced an amazing improvement in memory of over 10 years. In fact 30 days of taking ProceraAVH souped up their recall speed to the equivalant of a group just 31-35 years of age.

What's more, the ProceraAVH group showed improvements in a range of moods from feeling less anxious, confused and depressed to feeling more mental energy and clarity. However, what was soon to literally shock the audience was Dr. Stough's discovery that ProceraAVH also improved the group's IQ score, along with "fluid intelligence" and powers of reasoning. Dr. Stough, a world renown cognitive scientist and IQ researcher had never seen, or even heard of such a robust effect, especially since conventional wisdom holds that IQ is unchangeable.

To learn more about this landmark study, and the benefits and availability of ProceraAVH, go to www.BrainResearchLabs.com.

Appendix II

New Frontiers in Supplementation

Cognitive enhancement, both natural and pharmaceutical, is one of the most important and exciting new areas of scientific research. Here are some cognition-enhancing nutrients that are generally available and believed to be safe and effective:

ALPHA-GLYCERYLPHOSPHORYLCHOLINE (A-GPC) is a form of choline that gets to the brain quickly and supports ACh synthesis and membrane structure. A-GPC had been shown to improve impaired memory, and increase the body's production of human growth hormone (hGH). A-GPC may even have a neurotrophic effect, stimulating the growth of dendrites and possibly axons. Although more expensive than most choline precursors, it is more bioactive so less quantity is needed for a positive brain effect.

RHODIOLA (RHD) is an herbal supplement that appears to buffer the brain against the negative effects of stress, while actually improving cognitive performance. Once revealed as the secret behind the phenomenal strength and endurance feats of Bulgarian Olympic athletes, this high-altitude mountain plant is popular as an adaptogenic agent, specifically during times of stress or high-energy mental and physical performance demands.

SPANISH AND CHINESE SAGE (Salvia lavandulaefolia and Salvia miltiorrhiza) have been clinically shown to improve memory and possibly speed. Sage seems to acts in one or more ways to stimulate and support the ACh system. As a seasoning sage is great with turkey (the biggest herb in the stuffing), chicken, soups, and salad dressings.

FORSKOLIN (coleus forshohlii) is derived from the root of the coleus forshohlii plant. It activates the enzyme adenylate cyclase, which causes increased production of cyclic AMP (cAMP). cAMP is directly involved in the formation of long-term memory.

IDEBENONE is a synthetic molecule very similar to CoQ10 (ubiquinone). Idebenone increases nerve growth factor (NGF) in the brain, is a powerful antioxidant and neuroprotective agent, may improve information transfer between the right and left brain hemispheres, and can increase production of the brain neurotransmitters serotonin, dopamine, and norepinephrine, a brain energy and alertness neurotransmitter. Idebenone's main effect is on the mitochondria where its ATP energy-enhancing and neuroprotective effects are perhaps without equal. It is used in Europe to treat cognitive impairment. Idebenone is available from several reputable mail-order and Internet-based marketing companies.

GALANTAMINE improves memory, attention, and processing speed. Derived from several plants, including the snowdrop plant (Galanthus wornorii) and daffodils, galantamine has a dual action in the ACh system. It acts as an AChE inhibitor like HuperzineA and some FDA-approved drugs, such as Aricept (donepezil). It also stimulates the ACh nicotinic receptor. This makes it a powerful compound for the improvement of memory, mental clarity, and attention, especially in the aging or slightly impaired brain. Galantamine is available from several Internet-based marketing companies.

CDP-CHOLINE, OR CITICOLINE is a unique form of choline, which is very natural to the body since it is in a form the body already produces, readily passes through the blood-brain barrier where it enhances acetylcholine synthesis, strengthens cell membranes, and enhances cerebral metabolism and brain energy. Citicoline received a coveted award as one of the top new nutrients in the nutritional supplement industry in 2004.

Appendix III

New and Promising Pharmaceuticals for the Brain

In spite of the recent turmoil surrounding some of the large pharmaceutical companies and the horror stories associated with drugs like Vioxx, there are good medications which have been shown to improve brain health, performance, and longevity. Take ibuprofen, for example. Its anti-inflammatory action seems to be so strong that it even protects the brain from the neurodegenerative effects of most forms of brain inflammation. People taking ibuprofen may be significantly less likely to get Alzheimer's.

You can achieve much of these effects through a healthy brain diet, rich in anti-inflammatory foods, such as, the Omega-3 rich-fish and nuts, blueberries and pineapple, and the impressive turmeric spice. You can also use these anti-inflammatory supplements with certain medications, such as the antidiabetic drug pioglitazone, to reduce brain inflammation, lower glucose and cortisol levels, protect against insulin resistance, free radicals, and plaque formation in the brain. Note: always check with a physician before mixing medications with supplements.

The following are some of the medications available that can slow down brain aging and improve cognitive performance:

Metformin (Glucophage) is prescribed for diabetes. It is also a favorite drug in the antiaging community. It lowers insulin resistance, glucose levels, and inflammation. It is also believed to actually extend maximum lifespan (suggested by genetic DNA micro array tests).

Pioglitazone (Actos) and **Rosiglitazone (Avandia)** are also diabetic drugs used to increase insulin sensitivity via mechanistic actions different from Metformin. They work as PPARgamma agonists, and have been shown to down-regulate a variety of brain inflammatory mechanisms, including those caused by microglia and the Alzheimer's plaque, beta amyloid, or Abeta.

Anti-inflammatory medications such as Ibuprofen and Advil have been shown to reduce the risk of Alzheimer's.

Selegeline (deprenyl) acts as an MAO inhibitor and also shows powerful brain neuroprotective effects. It has been shown to improve the availability and the brain's utilization of dopamine.

Ergolid mesylates (Hydergine™) is a drug that was originally approved for senile dementia. Is believed to work as a nerve growth enzyme and very powerful neural antioxidant. It is more popular in Europe than in the United States. Unfortunately, it has not received the good press it deserves, perhaps because there are generic versions that diminish the pharmaceutical industry's incentive to advertise.

Statins (atorvastatin or Lipitor™; pravastatin or Pravachal™; simvastatin or Zocor™) have been reported to significantly lower (by up to 66 percent) the incidence of Alzheimers. Although it has been speculated that they reduce the harmful effects of excess cholesterol accumulation and its oxidation in the brain, other studies over the years suggest that statins may actually impair memory, perhaps due to their depletion of CoQ10, an important nutrient for the mitochondria. So if you take a statin, also take CoQ10 (100 to 300 mg./day).

Clioquinol (Mexaform, Oxychinol and Sterosan) is a class of antibiotics that also has the ability to reduce certain protein-metal biochemical interactions that are believed to cause soluble amyloids to form the dangerous insoluble Abeta plaques. The proposed mechanism is the chelation (removal) of the iron, zinc, and copper, thus blocking plaque formation that is dependent on these minerals.

Imatinib mesylate (Gleevec) is a leukemia drug that has also been shown to down-regulate (reduce) the formation of Abeta plaque, found in the brains of Alzheimer's patients.

RU-486 (French morning-after abortion pill) has been shown by Stanford, et al. to offset the effects of cortisol, known to kill the brain's learning and memory cells. Proposed as a new treatment for Alzheimer's, MCI (mild cognitive impairment) and AAMI (age associated memory impairment).

Rolipram, a drug normally prescribed for depression, has been found to improve memory and synaptic function in Alzheimer's transgenic mice. Its mechanism of action seems to be as an inhibitor of a phosphodiesterase, known as PDE4, which down-regulates a second messenger called cAMP. By inhibiting the action of PDE4, cAMP and CREB protein gene transcription are upregulated, improving the performance of the synapses for formation of long-term memory. Note: the natural herbal agent, Forskolin, also appears to render the same effects.

Cognitive Enhancers In Clinical Trials

Following is a brief list of a few pharmaceutical and nutraceutical agents that are undergoing clinical testing for use in Alzheimer's and possibly pre-Alzheimer states including MCI (mild cognitive impairment):

Ketasyn™ (AC-1202) is currently showing dramatic results in the treatment of Alzheimer's. Ketasyn is actually a beverage. The active ingredient is a compound traditionally sold (and still available) to body builders and athletes as MCT (medium chain triglyceride). The liver converts MCT to ketone bodies. These then enter the brain and provide an alternative source of energy for brain cells that no longer use glucose effectively. What's more, the compound may not only fire up ailing mitochondria and synapses, but also help fix the cerebral energy deficit that plagues the brain even in "normal" aging, let alone accelerated brain aging and many forms of neurodegenerative conditions, including Alzheimer's, Parkinson's, stroke and cerebral vascular disease.

Scyllo-inositol (AZD-103) is a drug made by Canadian biotech company, Transition Therapeutics that's now in Alzheimer's clinical trials. AZD-103 has shown promise in reducing the neuro-toxic amyloid beta (Abeta), soluble oligomers while improving cognitive performance in rats. Scyllo-inositol is similar but not exactly the same as a natural health food ingredient called, inositol. Phosphatidyl inositol is an active component of healthy brain cells membranes, and is known to aid in cellular calcium balance. Inositol has also been used to treat depression.

Dimebon was discovered in Russia and marketed there in 1983 as an antihistamine. In a recent randomized, double-blind, placebo-controlled study conducted in Russia by US based pharma company, Medivation Inc., Dimebon showed positive effects on all five clinical endpoints. Dimebon appears to have a unique double action of acting as both a cholinesterase inhibitor and an NMDA receptor antagonist. What's more, Dimebon is reported to inhibit neuronal death by protecting the mitochondria.

MEM 3454 is in a Phase 2 FDA trial. MEM 3454 is the proprietary product of Memory Pharmaceuticals., Inc. and has already been shown to improve memory in healthy, normal humans. MEM 3454 is a partial agonist of the nicotinic alpha-7 receptor, a highly specialized receptor found in the central nervous system (CNS). Compounds acting on this receptor may be beneficial in the treatment of Alzheimer's disease and schizophrenia, as well as other psychiatric and neurological disorders.

Sulbutiamine (SUL) (brand name: Arcalion®) is a precursor to thiamine (i.e., vitamin B1). Sulbutiamine has recently been shown to significantly enhance memory, especially when combined with an acetylcholinesterase inhibitor. SUL has been used by athletes and body builders to reduce fatigue and enhance workouts. It is available for over-the-counter sale as a nutritional supplement. Sulbutiamine's demonstrated ability to improve cognition suggests that it is a nootropic, or cognitive enhancer.

AMPAKINE® compounds are unique, proprietary, highly patented compounds from Cortex Pharmaceuticals, Inc., a public company, and have been proven to enhance memory, attention, alertness and other aspects of cognition. Cortex plans to use the Ampakines to target disorders ranging from early childhood, autism and Attention Deficit Hyperactivity Disorder to Baby Boomer and Elderly problems with age-associated memory impairment disorders, such as Alzheimer's disease, MCI and AAMI. The AMPAKINE® compounds enhance memory and cognition by acting on chemical pathways which impact at least 85% of all the neurotransmission occurring in the brain. Ampakines have been through considerable FDA sanctioned clinical testing and show great promise for treating a broad range of cognitive impairments, as well as cognitive enhancement in normal individuals.

Appendix IV

Medical Treatments

To date five drugs have been approved by the FDA for Alzheimer's disease.

Tacrine (Cognex™) – the first approved. Mechanism of action is the inhibition of acetylcholinesterase (an enzyme that attacks a primary memory neurotransmitter, acetylcholine). Not prescribed any longer because of side effects and stronger new drugs.

Donezepil (Aricept™) – the second approved acetylcholinesterase (AChE) inhibitor.

Rivastigmine (Exelon™) - the third approved AChE inhibitor.

Galantamine (Reminyl™) – a dual-action drug (originally derived from flower and herb sources), works as both an AChE inhibitor and nicotinic agonist (somewhat similar to the brain-stimulating effects of nicotine).

Mementine (Namenda™) is a new class of neuroprotective pharmacologic agents (NMDA antagonist) that works via a different mechanism, reducing the negative impact of excess glutamate (influx) in brain cells.

References

ABOUT COGNITIVE IMPAIRMENT—AGE ASSOCIATED MEMORY IMPAIRMENT (AAMI), MILD COGNITIVE IMPAIRMENT (MCI), AND ALZHEIMER'S

Bassuk, S.S., D. Wypij, and L.F. Berkman. 2000. Cognitive impairment and mortality in the community-dwelling elderly. *Am J Epidemiol* 151(7):676-99.

Morris, J. C. et al. 2001. Mild cognitive impairment represents early stage Alzheimer's disease. *Arch Neurol* 58(3):397-405.

Pavlik, V.N., et al. 2003. Relation between cognitive function and mortality in middle-aged adults: the atherosclerosis risk in communities study. *Am J Epidemiol* 157(4):327-34.

Petersen R., et al. 1999. Mild cognitive impairment. *Arch Neurol* 56:303-308

Brain Speed and Cognitive Impairment

Gordon, B., and K. Carson. 1990. The basis for choice reaction time slowing in Alzheimer's disease. *Brain Cogn* 13(2):148-66.

Muller, G., et al. 1991. Reaction time prolongation in the early stage of presenile onset Alzheimer's disease. *Eur Arch Psychiatry Clin Neurosc* 241(1):46-8.

Nebes, R.D., C.B. Brady, and C.F. Reynolds 3d. 1992. Cognitive slowing in Alzheimer's disease and geriatric depression. *J Gerontol* 47(5):331-36.

Nebes, R.D., and C.B. Brady. 1992. Generalized cognitive slowing and severity of dementia in Alzheimer's disease: implications for the interpretation of response-time data. *J Clin Exp Neuropsychol* 14(2):317-26.

Nebes, R.D., and D. J. Madden. 1988. Different patterns of cognitive slowing produced by Alzheimer's disease and normal aging. *Psychol Aging* 3(1):102-4.

Sano M., et al. 1995. Simple reaction time as a measure of global attention in Alzheimer's disease. *J Int Neuropsychol Soc* 1(1):56-61.

Smits, C. H., et al. 1999. Cognitive functioning and health as determinants of mortality in an older population. *Am J. Epidemiol* 150(9):978-86.

Zappoli R., et al. 1990. Cognitive event-related potentials and reaction time in presenile subjects with initial mild cognitive decline or probable Alzheimer-type dementia. *Ital J Neurol Sci* 11(2):113-30.

RISK FACTORS—AGE, FREE RADICALS, HYPERTENSION, DIABETES, CARDIOVASCU-LAR, HOMOCYSTEINE, CORTISOL, INSULIN RESISTANCE

Stress and Aging—Cortisol

Axelson, D., et al. 1993. Hypercortisolemia and hippocampal changes in depression.

Psychiatry Res 47:163-173.

Ferrari, E., et al. 2001. Age-related changes of the hypothalamic-pituitary-adrenal axis: patho-physiological correlates. *EurJ Endocrinol* 144(4):319-29 0804-4.

Herman, J.P., and W. E. Cullinan. 1997. Neurocircuitry of stress: central control of the hypothal-amo-pituitary-adrenocortical axis. *Trends Neurosci* 20:78-84.

Isovich E., M.J. Flugge, and M.J. Mijnster. 2000. Chronic psychosocial stress reduces the density of dopamine transporters. *Eur J Neurosci* 12(3):1071-8.

Kalmijn, S., et al. 1998. A prospective study on cortisol, dehydroepiandrosterone sulfate (DHEAs), and cognitive function in the elderly. *J Clin Endocrinol Metab* 83(10):3487-92.

Kirschbaum, C., et al. 1996. Stress- and treatment-induced elevations of cortisol levels associat-ed with impaired verbal and spatial declarative memory in healthy adults. *Life Sci* 48: 1475-146.

Leblhuber, F., et al. 1993. Age and sex differences of dehydroepiandrosterone sulfate (DHEAS) and cortisol (CRT). Plasma levels in normal controls and Alzheimer's disease (AD)

Psycholpharmacology 111(1):23-26.

Lupien, S.J., et al. 1998. Cortisol levels during human aging predict hippocampal atrophy and memory deficits. *Nature Neuroscience* 1(1):69-73.

Lupien, S.J., et al. 1999. Increased cortisol levels and impaired cognition in human aging: impli-cation for depression and dementia in later life. *Rev Neurosci* 10(2):117-39.

Magariños, A.M., et al. 1996. Chronic psychosocial stress causes apical dendritic atrophy of hip-pocampal CA3 pyramidal neurons in subordinate tree shrews. *J Neurosci* 16(10):3534-40.

MacLullich AM, Deary IJ, Starr JM, Ferguson KJ, Wardlaw JM, Seckl JR. 2005. Plasma cortisol levels, brain volumes and cognition in healthy elderly men. *Psychoneuroendocrinology*.30(5):505-15

Newcomer, J.W. 1999. Decreased memory performance in healthy humans induced by stress-level cortisol treatment. *Arch Gen Psychiatry* 56(6):527-33.

Richards, J., and J. Gross. 1999. Suppression of emotion impairs memory. Reuters

Personality and Social Psychology Bulletin 25:1003-1044.

Sapolsky, R. M. 1996. Why stress is bad for your brain. *Science* 273:49-50.

Free Radicals and Oxidative Stress

Albers, D.S. 2000. Mitochondrial dysfunction and oxidative stress in aging and neurodegenerative disease. *J Neural Trans* 59(S):133-54.

Ames, B.N., and M. K. Shigenaga. 1992. Oxidants are a major contributor to aging. *Ann N Y Acad Sci* 663:85-96.

Beckman, K. B., and B. N. Ames. 1998. The free radical theory of aging matures. *Physiol Rev* 78(2):547-81.

Berr, C., et al. 1998. Systemic oxidative stress and cognitive performance in the population-based EVA study. *Free Radic Biol Med* 24(7-8):1202-8.

Cardoso, S.M. 1999. Mitochondrial function is differentially affected by oxidative stress. *Free Radical Biology & Medicine* 26(1-2):3-13.

Cocco, T. 1999. Arachidonic acid interaction with mitochondrial electron transport chain promotes reactive oxygen species (free radical) generation. *Free Radical Biology & Medicine* 27(1/2): 51-59.

De al Monte, S. M., et al. 2000. Mitochondrial DNA damage as a mechanism of cell loss in Alzheimer's disease. *Lab Invest* 80(8):1323-35.

Halliwell, B. 2001. Role of free radicals in the neurodegenerative diseases: therapeutic implications for antioxidant treatment. *Drugs Aging* 18(9):685-716.

Jonnala, R. R., and J. J. Buccafusco. 2001. Inhibition of nerve growth factor by peroxynitrite. *J. Neurosci Res* 63(1):27-34.

Olanow, C. W., and G. W. Arendash. 1994. Metals and free radicals in neurodegeneration.

Curr Opin Neurol 7(6):548-58.

Pratico, D., et al. 2002. Increase of brain oxidative stress in mild cognitive impairment: a possible predictor of Alzheimer disease. *Arch Neurol* 59(6):972-6.

Sastre, J., F. V. Pallardo, and J. Vina. 2000. Mitochondrial oxidative stress plays a key role in aging and apoptosis. *IUBMB Life* 49(5):427-35.

Tabet, N., D. Mantle, and M. Orrell. 2000. Free radicals as mediators of toxicity in Alzheimer's disease: a review and hypothesis. *Adverse Drug React Toxicol Rev* 19(2):127-52.

Tritschler, H.J., L. Packer, and R. Medori. 1994. Oxidative stress and mitochondrial dysfunction in neurodegeneration. *Biochem Mol Biol Int* 34(1):169-81.

Genetic Factors

Gibson, G. 2000. Mitochondrial damage in Alzheimer's disease varies with apoliprotein E genotype. *Ann Neurol* 48:297-303.

Haan, M. 1999. The role of APOE e4 as risk factor risk for cognitive decline. *JAMA* 282:40-46

Effects of Glucose/Insulin Dysfunction—High-Glycemic Diet, AGEs

Ho, L. et al. 2004. Diet-induced insulin resistance promotes amyloidosis in a transgenic mouse model of Alzheimer's disease. *FASEB J* 18:902-4.

Kalmijn, S., et al. 1995. Glucose intolerance, hyperinsulinaemia and cognitive function in a general population of elderly men. *Diabetologia* 38(9):1096-102.

Messier, C, and M. Gagnon. 2000. Glucose regulation and brain aging. *J Nutr Health Aging* 4(4):208-13.

Perlmutter, L.C., et al. 1984. Decreased cognitive function in aging non-insulin-dependent diabetic patients. *Amer J Medicine* 77(6):1043-8.

Vitek, M. P., et al. 1994. Advanced glycation end products contribute to amyloidosis in Alzheimer's disease. *Proc Natl Acad Sci* 91:4766-770.

Homocysteine

Clarke, R. 1998. Folate, vitamin B, and serum total homocysteine levels in confirmed Alzheimer's disease. *Arch Neurol* 55(11):1449-55.

Dufouil, C., et al. 2003. Homocysteine, white matter hyperintensities, and cognition in healthy elderly people. *Ann Neurol* 53(2):214-21.

Da Costa, K. A., et al. 2005. Choline deficiency in mice and humans is associated with increased plasma homocysteine concentration after a methionine load. *Am J Clin Nutr* 81:440-444.

Hirsch, S., et al. 2002. Hyperhomocysteinemia and endothelial function in young subjects: effects of vitamin supplementation. *Clin Cardiol* 25(11):495-501.

Selhub, J. 2000. B vitamins, homocysteine, and neurocognitive function in the elderly. *Am J Clin Nutr* 71(2):614S-20S.

Teunissen, C. E., et al. 2003. Homocysteine: a marker for cognitive performance? A longitudinal follow-up study. *J Nutr Health Aging* 7(3):153-9.

Hypertension

Bellew, K. M., et al. 2004. Hypertension and the rate of cognitive decline in patients with dementia of the Alzheimer type. *Alzheimer Dis Assoc Disord* 18(4):208-213.

DeCarli, C. 1999. Mild hypertension in midlife speeds aging of brain. *Stroke* 30:529-536.

Kilander, L., et al. 1998. Hypertension is related to cognitive impairment: a 20-year follow-up of 999 men. *Hypertension* 31(3):780-6.

Kalmijn, S. 2000. High blood pressure, cholesterol and weight increase dementia risk. American Academy of Neurology's 52nd Annual Meeting in San Diego, CA

Kivipelto, M., et al. 2001. Midlife vascular risk factors and late-life mild cognitive impairment: *Neurology* 26;56(12):1683-9.

Knopman, D., et al. 2001. Cardiovascular risk factors and cognitive decline in middle-aged adults. *Neurology* 56(a):42-8.

Inflammation

Berger, A. 2000. Inflammation and Alzheimer's disease. *Neurobiol Aging* 21(3):383-421.

Finch, C. E., 2005. Developmental origins of aging in brain and blood vessels: an overview. *Neurobiol Aging* 26(3):281-91.

McGeer, E. G., and P. L. McGeer. 1999. Brain inflammation in Alzheimer disease and the therapeutic implications. *Current Pharmaceutical Design* 5(10):821-36.

Stanimirovic, D., and K. Satoh. 2000. Inflammatory mediators of cerebral endothelium; a role in ischemic brain inflammation. *Brain Pathol* 10(1):13-26.

Insulin Resistance

Ho, L., et al. 2004. Diet-induced insulin resistance promotes amyloidosis in a transgenic mouse model of Alzheimer's disease. *FASEB J* 18:902-4.

Other

Jaffe, K. 1999. Osteoporosis may be linked to mental decline. Reuters. *J Amer Geriatrics Soc* 47:1176-1182.

Richards, J., and J. Gross. 1999. Suppression of emotion impairs memory. Reuters *Personality and Social Psychology Bulletin* 25:1003-1044.

Prevention and Treatment

Breitner, J.C.S., 1996. The role of anti-inflammatory drugs in the prevention and treatment of Alzheimer's disease. *Ann Rev Med* 47:401–411.

Breitner, J.C.S., et al. 1995. Delayed onset of Alzheimer's disease with non-steroidal anti-inflammatory and histamine H2 blocking drugs. *Neurobiol Aging* 16(4):523–530.

Calon, F., et al. 2004. Docosahexaenoic acid protects from dendritic pathology in an Alzheimer's disease mouse model. *Neuron* 43(5):633-45.

Koudinov, A. R., et al. 1999. HDL phospholipid: a natural inhibitor of Alzheimer's amyloid beta-fibrillogenesis? *Clin Chem Lab Med* 37(10):993-4.

Lleó, A., et al. 2004. Nonsteroidal anti-inflammatory drugs lower Abeta(42) and change presenilin 1 conformation. *Nat Med* 10(10):1065-6.

Maelicke, A. 2000. Allosteric modulation of nicotinic receptors as a treatment strategy for Alzheimer's disease. *Cognitive Discord* 11(S1):11-18.

Newman, P.E., 1998. Could diet be used to reduce the risk of developing Alzheimer's disease? *Med Hypothesis* 50(4):335-7.

Solfrizzi, V. 1999. High monounsaturated fatty acids intake protects against age-related cognitive decline. *Neurology 52:*156-1569.

Pharmaceutical Agents for Improvement of Cognitive Performance

Adams, W. 1982. Effect of methylphenidate on thought processing time in children. *J Dev Behav Pediatr* 3(3):133-5.

Hasbroucq, T., P. Rihet, and C. A. Possamai. 1997. Serotonin and human information processing: fluvoxamin can improve reaction time performance. *Neuroscience Letter* 4;229(3):204-8.

Pavlik, A., and J. Pilar. 1989. Protection of cell proteins against free-radical attack by nootropic drugs: scavenger effect of pyritinol confirmed by electron spin resonance spectroscopy. *Neuropharmacology* 28(6):557-61.

Wagstaff, L. R., et al. 2003. Statin-associated memory loss: analysis of 60 case reports and review of the literature. *Pharmacotherapy* 23(7):871-80.

Zobel, A. W., et al. 2004. Improvement of working but not declarative memory is correlated with HPA normalization during antidepressant treatment. *J Psychiatr Res* 38(4):377-83.

ENVIRONMENTAL—NEUROTOXINS, HEAVY METALS, HEAD INJURIES, LIFESTYLE FACTORS, INFECTION

Langford D, Masliah E. The emerging role of infectious pathogens in neurodegenerative diseases. Exp Neurol. 2003 Dec ;184(2):553-5.

Olanow, C. W., and G. W. Arendash. 1994. Metals and free radicals in neurodegeneration. *Curr Opin Neurol* 7(6):548-58.

Aluminum

Paik, S. R.,1997. Aluminum-induced structural alterations of the precursor of the non-A beta component of Alzheimer's disease amyloid. *Arch Biochem Biophys* 15:344(2):325-34.

Rao, J. K. 1998. Experimental aluminum encephalomyelopathy. Relationship to human neurodegenerative disease. *Clin Lab Med 18*(4):687-98.

Head Injuries

Azouvi, P., et al. 1996. Working memory and supervisory control after severe closed-head injury. A study of dual task performance and random generation. *J Clin Exo Neuropsychol* 18(3):317-37.

Smith, D. H., et al. 1999. Accumulation of amyloid beta and tau and the formation of neurofilament inclusions following diffuse brain injury in the pig. *J Neuropathol Exp Neurol* 58(9):982-92.

Infections

Langford, D., and E. Masliah. 2003. The emerging role of infectious pathogens in neurodegenerative diseases. Exp *Neurol* 184(2):553-5.

Shor, A. 1999. Chlamydia pneumoniae bacteria role in atherosclerosis. *JAMA* 282:2071-73.

Iron

Rouault, T. 2001. Abnormal iron deposits may cause some brain disorders. *Nature Genetics 27:209-214.*

Lead

Tong, S., et al. 1996. Lifetime exposure to environmental lead and children's intelligence at 11-13 years: the Port Pirie cohort study. *Brit Med J* 312(7046):1569-75.

Tong, S., Y. E. von Schirnding, and T. Prapamontol. 2000. Environmental lead exposure: a public health problem of global dimensions. *Bull World Health Organ* 78(9):1068-77.

Stollery, B. T. 1996. Reaction time changes in workers exposed to lead. *Neurotoxicol Teratol* 18(4):477-83.

Mercury

Hock, C., et al. 1998. Increased blood mercury levels in patients with Alzheimer's disease. *J Neural Transm* 105(1):59-68.

Pendergrass, J. C., et al. 19987. Mercury vapor inhalation inhibits binding of GTP to tubulin in rat brain: similarity to a molecular lesion in Alzheimer diseased brain. *Neurotoxicology* 18(2):315-24.

HEALTHY FOOD AND DIET—ANTIOXIDANT AND ANTI-INFLAMMATORY EFFECTS OF RED WINE, BERRIES, SPICES, GREENS AND VEGETABLES, FISH OIL

Breteler, M. 2000. Diet may prevent Alzheimer's disease. *6th International Stockholm-Springfield Symposium, Sweden.*

Cao, G., E. Sofic, and R. L. Prior. 1996. Antioxidant capacity of tea and common vegetables.

J Agric Food Chem 44:3426-3431.

Capurso, A. 1999. Mediterranean diet can help prevent memory loss. *Neurology* 52:1563-1569.

David, J. A., et al. 2005. Direct comparison of a dietary portfolio of cholesterol-lowering foods with a statin in hypercholesterolemic participants. *Am J Clin Nutr* 81:380-387.

Engelhart, M. J., et al. 2002. Dietary intake of antioxidants and risk of Alzheimer disease. *JAMA* 287(24):3223-9.

Franco, O. H., et al. 2004. The Polymeal: a more natural, safer, and probably tastier (than the Polypill) strategy to reduce cardiovascular disease by more than 75%. *BMJ* 329:1.

Halliwell, B. 2001. Role of free radicals in the neurodegenerative diseases: therapeutic implications for antioxidant treatment. *Drugs Aging* 18(9):685-716.

Joseph, J. 1998. Antioxidants in fruit, vegetables slow brain aging. *J Neuroscience* 18.

Newman, P.E. 1998. Could diet be used to reduce the risk of developing Alzheimer's disease? *Med Hypothesis* 50(4):335-7.

Perrig, W. J., P. Perrig, and H. B. Stahelin. 1997. The relation between antioxidants and memory performance in the old and very old. *J Am Geriatr Soc* 45(6)718-24.

Prior, R. L., 2003. Fruits and vegetables in the prevention of cellular oxidative damage *Amer J of Clinical Nutrition* 78(3):570S-578S.

Youdim, K. A., A. Martin, and J. A. Joseph. 2000. Essential fatty acids and the brain: possible health benefits. *Int J Dev Neurosci* 8(4-5):383-99.

Zandi, P. P., et al. 2004. Reduced risk of Alzheimer disease in users of antioxidant vitamin supplements: the cache county study [In Process Citation] *Arch Neurol* 61(1):82-8.

Boron

Penland, J. G., 1994. Dietary boron, brain function, and cognitive performance. *Environ Health Perspect* 102(S):7:65-72.

Berries, Grapes

Joseph, J. A., B. Shukitt-Hale, and G. Casadesus, 2005. Reversing the deleterious effects of aging on neuronal communication and behavior: beneficial properties of fruit polyphenolic compounds. *Am J Clin Nutr* ;81(1):313S-6S.

Joseph, J. A., et al. 1999. Reversals of age-related declines in neuronal signal transduction, cognitive, and motor behavioral deficits with blueberry, spinach, or strawberry dietary supplementation. *J Neurosci* 19(18):8114-2121.

Joseph, J. A., et al. 1998. Long-term dietary strawberry, spinach, or vitamin E supplementation retards the onset of age-related neuronal signal-transduction and cognitive behavioral deficits. *J of Neurosci* 18(19):8047-55.

Joseph, J. 1999. Blueberries reverse signs of aging in rats. *J Neurosci* 19:8114-8121.

Joseph, J. A., et al. 2003. Blueberry supplementation enhances signaling and prevents behavioral deficits in an Alzheimer disease model. *Nutritional Neuroscience* 6:153-162.

Wang, H., G. Cao, and R. L. Prior. 1997. Oxygen radical absorbing capacity of anthocyanins. *J Agric Food Chem* 45:304-309.

Caloric Restriction

Kim, D. W., 2000. Effects of age and dietary restriction on animal model SAMP8 mice with learning and memory impairments. *J Nutr Health Aging* 4(4):233-8.

Lee, C. K., and R. Weindruch, R. 2000. Skip the calories and save your brain. *Nature Genetics* 25:294-297.

Lee, J., et al. 2000. Dietary restriction increases the number of newly generated neural cells, and induces BDNF expression, in the dentate gyrus of rats. *J Mol Neurosci.* 15(2):99-108.

Caffeine

Jarvis, M. J. 1993. Does caffeine intake enhance absolute levels of cognitive performance? *Psychopharmacology* 110(1-2):45-52.

Fish

Calon, F., et al. 2004. Docosahexaenoic acid protects from dendritic pathology in an Alzheimer's disease mouse model. *Neuron* 43(5):633-45.

Ellis, E. F., et al. 1990. Effect of fish oil n-3 acid on cerebral microcirculation. *J Physiol* 258(6):H1780-05.

Kalmijn, S., et al. 2004. Dietary intake of fatty acids and fish in relation to cognitive performance at middle age. *Neurology* 27;62(2):275-80.

Whalley, L. J., et al. 2004. Cognitive aging, childhood intelligence, and the use of food supplements: possible involvement of n–3 fatty acids. *Am J Clin Nutr* 80:1650-1657.

Vitamin E

Morris, M. C., et al. 2005. Relation of the tocopherol forms to incident Alzheimer disease and to cognitive change. *Am J Clin Nutr* 81:508-514.

Eggs—Organic, Free-Range, DHA, and Vitamin E-Enriched

Ferrier, L. K., et al. 1995. Alpha-linolenic acid- and docosahexaenoic acid-enriched eggs from hens fed flaxseed: influence on blood lipids and platelet phospholipid fatty acids in humans. *Am J Clin Nutr* 62(1):81-6.

Kritchevsky, S. B., and D. Kritchevsky D. 2000. Egg consumption and coronary heart disease: an epidemiologic overview. *J Am Coll Nutr* 19(5 S):549S-555S.

Lucas, A., 1998. Diet of preterm infants affects subsequent cognitive function. *BMJ* 317;1481-1487.

Makrides, M., et al. 2002. Nutritional effect of including egg-yolk in the weaning diet of breast-fed and formula-fed infants: a randomized clinical trial. *Am J Clin Nutr* 75:1084-1092.

Olive Oil

Capurso, A. 1999. High levels of monounsaturated fatty acid intake protects against age-related memory loss. *Neurology* 52:1563-1569.

Solfrizzi, V. 1999. High monounsaturated fatty acids intake protects against age-related cognitive decline. *Neurology* 52:1563-1569.

Red Bell Pepper

Suganuma, H. 1999. Amelioratory effects of dietary ingestion with red bell pepper on learning impairment in senescence-accelerated mice (SAMP8). *Jou Nutr Sci Vitaminol* 45(1):143-9.

Spinach

Joseph, J. A., B. Shukitt-Hale, and G. Casadesus. 2005. Reversing the deleterious effects of aging on neuronal communication and behavior: beneficial properties of fruit polyphenolic compounds. *Am J Clin Nutr* 81(1):313S-6S.

Joseph, J.A., et al. 1999. Reversals of age-related declines in neuronal signal transduction, cognitive, and motor behavioral deficits with blueberry, spinach, or strawberry dietary supplementation. *J Neurosci* 19(18):8114-21.

Joseph, J.A., et al. 1998. Long-term dietary strawberry, spinach, or vitamin E supplementation retards the onset of age-related neuronal signal-transduction and cognitive behavioral deficits. *J Neurosci* 18:8047.

Walnuts

Zambon, D. 2000. Walnuts may help lower harmful cholesterol. *Annals of Internal Medicine* 132:538-546.

Whey Protein Powder

Markus, C. R., 2000. The whey protein alpha-lactalbumin increases the plasma ratio of typtophan to the other large neutral amino acids, and in vulnerable subjects raises brain serotonin activity, reduces cortisol concentration, and improves mood under stress. *Amer J of Clinical Nutrition* 71(6):1536-1544.

Anti-Oxidant/Neuroprotective Herbal Seasonings and Spices

Choi, H. R., et al. 2002. Peroxynitrite scavenging activity of herb extracts. *Phytother Res* 16(4):364-7.

Das, K.C., and C. K. Das. 2002. Curcumin (diferuloylmethane), a singlet oxygen (O-1(2)) quencher. *Biochem Biophys Res Commun* 295(1):62–66.

Kosaka K, and T. Yokoi. 2003. Carnosic acid, a component of rosemary (rosmarinus officinalis L.), promotes synthesis of nerve growth factor in T98G human glioblastoma cells. *Biol Pharm Bull* 26(11):1620-2.

Lim, G. P., et al. 2001. The curry spice curcumin reduces oxidative damage and amyloid pathology in an Alzheimer transgenic mouse. *J Neurosci* 21(21):8370-7.

Moss, M., et al. 2003. Aromas of rosemary and lavender essential oils differentially affect cognition and mood in healthy adults. *Int J Neurosci* 113(1):15-38.

Ono, K., et al. 2004. Curcumin has potent anti-amyloidogenic effects for Alzheimer's beta-amyloid fibrils in vitro. *J Neurosci Res* 15:75(6):742-50.

Ozcan, M. 2003. Antioxidant activities of rosemary, sage, and sumac extracts and their combinations on stability of natural peanut oil. *J Med Food* 6(3):267-70.

Park, S. Y., and D. S. Kim. 2002. Discovery of natural products from Curcuma longa that protect cells from beta-amyloid insult: a drug discovery effort against Alzheimer's disease. *J Nat Prod* 65(9):1227-31.

Tildesley, N. T., et al. 2003. Salvia lavandulaefolia (Spanish sage) enhances memory in healthy young volunteers. *Pharmacol Biochem Behav* 75(3):669-74.

Yang F., et al. 2004. Curcumin inhibits formation of Abeta oligomers and fibrils and binds plaques and reduces amyloid in vivo. *J Biol Chem* 280(7):5892-901.

NUTRITIONAL SUPPLEMENTS—NEUROPROTECTIVE AND COGNITIVE ENHANCING

Acetyl-L-Carnitine and Carnitine

Athanassakis, I. 2002. L-carnitine accelerates the in vitro regeneration of neural network from adult murine brain cells. *Brain Res* 932:70-78.

Arockia Rani, P. J., and C. Panneerselvam. 2001. Carnitine as a free radical scavenger in aging. *Exp Gerontol* 36(10):1713-26.

Ando, S., et al. 2001. Enhancement of learning capacity and cholinergic synaptic function by carnitine in aging rats. *J Neurosci Res* 66(2):266-71.

Arrigo, A. 1990. Effects of acetyl-L-carnitine on reaction times in patients with cerebrovascular insufficiency. *Int J Clin Pharmacol Res* 10(1-2):133-137.

Binienda ZK. 2003. Neuroprotective effects of L-carnitine in induced mitochondrial dysfunction. *Ann N Y Acad Sci* (United States) 993 p289-95

Brooks, J. O., et al. 1998. Acetyl-L-carnitine slows decline in younger patients with Alzheimer's disease: a reanalysis of a double-blind, placebo-controlled study using the trilinear approach. *Int Psychogeriatric* 10(2):193-203.

Calvani, M., and E. Arrigoni-Martelli. 1999. Attenuation by acetyl-L-carnitine of neurological damage and biochemical derangement following brain ischemia and reperfusion. *Int J Tissue React* 21(1):1-6.

Hagen,T. M., C. M. Wehr, and B. N. Ames. 1998. Mitochondrial decay in aging: reversal through supplementation of acetyl-L-carnitine and N-tert-butyl-alphaphenyl-nitrone. *Ann NY Acad Sci* 854:214-223.

Hagen, T.M., et al. 1998. Acetyl-L-carnitine fed to old rats partially restores mitochondrial function and ambulatory activity. *Proc Natl Acad Sci* 95:9562-66.

Liu, J. et al. 2002. Memory loss in old rats is associated with brain mitochondrial decay and RNA/DNA oxidation: partial reversal by feeding acetyl-L-carnitine and/or R-alpha-lipoic acid. *Proc Natl Acad Sci* 99(4):2356-61.

Montgomery, S. A., L. J. Thal, and R. Amrein. 2003. Meta-analysis of double blind randomized controlled clinical trials of acetyl-L-carnitine versus placebo in the treatment of mild cognitive impairment and mild Alzheimer's disease. *Int Clin Psychopharmacol* 18(2):61-71.

Murray, M. T., 1996. The many benefits of carnitine. *Am J Nat Med* 3(2):6-14.

Pettegrew, J. W. 1995. Clinical and neurochemical effects of acetyl-Lcarnitine in Alzheimer's disease. *Neurobiol Aging* 16(1):1-4.

Piovesan, P., et al. 1994. Acetyl L-carnitine treatment increases choline acetytransferase activity and NGF levels in the CNS of adult rats following total fimbria-fornix transection. *Brain Research* 633(1-2):77-82.

Savioli, G., and M. Neri. 1994. L-acetylcarnitine treatment of mental decline in the elderly. *Drugs Exp Clin Res* 20(4):169-176.

Sershen, H. et al. 1991. Effect of acetyl-L-carnitine on the dopaminergic system in aging brain. *J Neurosci Res* (3):555-9.

Sharman EH, Vaziri ND, Ni Z, et al. 2002. Reversal of biochemical and behavioral parameters of brain aging by melatonin and acetyl L-carnitine. *Brain Res* (Netherlands) 957(2) p223-30

Tempesta, E. et al. 1990. Role of acetyl-L-carnitine in the treatment of cognitive deficit in chronic alcoholism. *Int J Clin Pharmacol Res* 10(1-2):101-107.

Virmani, M. A. 1995. Protective actions of L-carnitine and acetyl-L-carnitine on the neurotoxicity evoked by mitochondrial uncoupling or inhibitors. *Pharmacol Res* 32:383-389.

White, H. L. 1990. Acetyl-L-carnitine as a precursor of acetylcholine. *Neurochem Res* 15:597-601.

Alpha Lipoic Acid

Liu, J. et al. 2002. Memory loss in old rats is associated with brain mitochondrial decay and RNA/DNA oxidation: partial reversal by feeding acetyl-L-carnitine and/or R-alpha -lipoic acid.

Proc Natl Acad Sci 99(4):2356-61.

Hagen, T.M., 1999. (R)-alpha-lipoic acid-supplemented old rats have improved mitochondrial function, decreased oxidative damage, and increased metabolic rate. *FASEB J* 13(2):411-18.

Parker, L., et al. 1997. Neuroprotection by the metabolic antioxidant alpha-lipoic acid. *Free Radical Biol Med* 22(1-2):359-78.

Stroll, S., et al. 1993. The potent free radical scavenger alpha-lipoic acid improved memory in aged mice: putative relationship to NMDA receptor deficits. *Pharmacol Biochem Behav* 46(4):799-805.

Vitamin A and Derivatives

Den Heijer, T., et al. 2001. Serum carotenoids and cerebral white matter lesions: the Rotterdam scan study. *J Am Geriatr Soc* 49(5):642-6.

Kheir-Eldin, A. A., et al. 2001. Protective effect of vitamin E, beta-carotene and N-acetylcysteine from the brain oxidative stress induced in rats by lipopolysaccharide. *Int J Biochem Cell Biol* 33(5):475-82.

Takahasho, J. 1999. Retinoic acid and neurotrophins collaborate to regulate neurogenesis in adult-derived neural stem cell cultures. *J Neurobiol* 38(1):65-81.

B Vitamins

Benton, D., R. Griffiths, and J. Haller. 1997. Thiamine supplementation mood and cognitive functioning. *Psychopharmocology* 129(1):66-71.

Bernard, M. A., P. A. Nakonezny, and T. M. Kasdhner. 1998. The effects of vitamin B12 deficiency on older veterans and its relationship to health. *J Am Geriatr Soc* 46:1199-1206.

Chong, Z. Z., S. H. Lin, and K. Maiese. 2002. Nicotinamide modulates mitochondrial membrane potential and cysteine protease activity during cerebral vascular endothelial cell injury. *J Vasc Res* 39(2):131-47.

Erb, C., and J. Klein. 1998. Enhancement of brain choline levels by nicotinamide: mechanism of action. *Neurosci Lett* 249:111-114.

Kamat, J. P., and T. P. Devasagayam. 1999. Nicotinamide (vitamin B3) as an effective antioxidant against oxidative damage in rat brain mitochondria. *Redox Rep* 4(4):179-84.

Maiese, K., and Z. Z. Chong. 2003. Nicotinamide: necessary nutrient emerges as a novel cytoprotectant for the brain. *Trends Pharmacol Sci* 24(5):228-32.

Mukherjee, S. K., and Adams, J. D. 1997. The effects of aging and neurodegeneration on apoptosis-associated DNA fragmentation. And the benefits of nicotinamide (vitamin B-3). *Mol Chem Neuropathol* 32(1-3):59-74.

Nilsson, K., L. Gustafson, and B. Hultberg. 2001. Improvement of cognitive functions after cobalamin/folate supplementation in elderly patients with dementia and elevated plasma homocysteine. *Int J Geriatr Psych* 16:609-614.

Robins Wahlin, T. B., et al. 2001. The influence of serum vitamin B12 and folate status on cognitive functioning in very old age. *Biol Pschol* 56(3):247-65.

Sheng, Y., et al. 1998. DNA repair enhancement by a combined supplement of carotenoids, nicotinamide, and zinc. *Cancer Detect Prev* 22(4):284-92.

Snowdon, D. A., et al. Serum folate and the severity of atrophy of the neocortex in Alzheimer disease: findings from the Nun study. *Am J Clin Nutr* ;71(4):993-8.

Yang J., et al. 2004. Early administration of nicotinamide prevents learning and memory impairment in mice induced by 1-methyl-4-phenyl-1, 2, 3, 6-tetrahydropyridine [In Process Citation] *Pharmacol Biochem Behav* 78(1):179-83.

Boron

Penland, J. G. 1994. Dietary boron, brain function, and cognitive performance. *Environ Health Perspect* 102(S7):65-72.

Choline and Phosphatidyl choline

Blusztajn, J. 1998. Choline, a vital amine. *Science* Vol 281:794-795.

Furey, M. L., P. Pietrini, and J. V. Hazby. 2000. Cholinergic enhancement and increased selectivity of perceptual processing during working memory. *Science* 22:290(5500):2315-9.

Furey, M. L., et al. 1997. Cholinergic stimulation alters performance and task-specific regional cerebral blood flow during working memory. *Proc Natl Acad Sci* 94(12):6512-6.

Da Costa, K. A., et al. 2005. Choline deficiency in mice and humans is associated with increased plasma homocysteine concentration after a methionine load. *Am J Clin Nutr* 81: 440-444.

Sitaram, M., H. Weingartner, and J. C. Gillin. 1978. Human serial learning: enhancement with choline and impairment with scopolamine. *Science* 201:274-276.

Zeisel, S. H. 1992. Choline: an important nutrient in brain development, liver function and carciogenesis. *J Am Coll Nutr* 11(5):473-81.

Zeisel, S. H. 2000. Choline: needed for normal development of memory. *Amer Coll Nutr* 528S-531S.

Zeisel, S. H. 1997. Choline; essential for brain development and function. *Adv Pediatr* 44:263-95.

Creatine

Rae, C., et al. 2003. Oral creatine monohydrate supplementation improves brain performance: a double-blind, placebo-controlled, cross-over trial. *Proc R Soc Lond B Biol Sci* 22:270(1529):2147-50.

Vitamin C

Heitzer, T. 2001. Beneficial effects of alpha-lipoic acid and ascorbic acid on endothelium-dependent, nitric oxide-mediated vasodilation in diabetic patients: relation to parameters of oxidative stress. *Free Radic Biol Med* 31:53-61.

Ling, L., et al. 2002. Vitamin C preserves endothelial function in patients with coronary heart disease after a high-fat meal. *Clin Cardiol* 25(5):219-24.

Masaki, K. 2000. Vitamin C, E may protect the aging brain. Reuters. *Neurology* 54:1265-1272.

Zandi PP, Anthony JC, Khachaturian AS, et al. 2004.Reduced risk of Alzheimer disease in users of antioxidant vitamin supplements: the Cache County Study. *Arch Neurol*), 61(1) p82-8

Carnosine

Hipkiss, A. R., and C. Brownson. 2000. A possible new role for the anti-aging peptide carnosine. *Cell Mol Life Science* 57(5):747-53.

Wang, A. M., et al. 2000. Use of carnosine as a natural anti-senescence drug for human beings. *Biochemistry* 65(7):869-71.

Boldyrev, A. A., et al. 1997. Biochemical and physiological evidence that carnosine is a neuro-protector against free radicals. *Cell Mol Neurobiol* 17(2):259-71.

DHEA

Hu Y, Cardounel A, Gursoy E, et al. 2000. Anti-stress effects of dehydroepiandrosterone: protection of rats against repeated immobilization stress-induced weight loss, glucocorticoid receptor production, and lipid peroxidation. *Biochem Pharmacol* (England) 59(7) p753-62

Morales, A. J., et al. 1998. The effects of six months treatment with a 100 mg daily dose of dehydroepiandrosterone (DHEA) on circulating sex steroids, body composition and muscle strength in age-advanced men and women. *Clin Endocrinol* 49(4):421-432.

Schmidt, P. J., et al. 2005. Dehydroepiandrosterone monotherapy in midlife-onset major and minor depression. *Arch Gen Psychiatry.* 62(2):154-62.

Van Niekerk, J.K., F. A. Huppert, and J. Herbert. 2001. Salivary cortisol and DHEA: association with measures of cognition and well-being in normal older men, and effects of three months of DHEA supplementation. *Psychoneuroendocrinology* 26(6):591-612.

DHA — Fish Oil

Kalmijn, S., et al. 2004. Dietary intake of fatty acids and fish in relation to cognitive performance at middle age. *Neurology* 62(2):275-80.

Kitajka, K., et al. 2002. The role of n-3 polyunsaturated fatty acids in brain: modulation of rat brain gene expression by dietary n-3 fatty acids. *Proc Natl Acad Sci* 99:2619-2624.

Gamoh, S., et al. Chronic administration of docosahexaenoic acid improves reference memory-related learning ability in young rats. *Neuroscience* 93(1):237-41.

Sazaki, T., et al. 2000. Anti-stress effects of DHA. *Biofactors* 13(1-4):41-5 0951-6433.

Whalley, L. J., et al. 2004. Cognitive aging, childhood intelligence, and the use of food supplements: possible involvement of n–3 fatty acids. *Am J Clin Nutr* 80(6):1650-1657.

Vitamin E and Coenzyme Q10

Barbiroli, B., et al. 1997. Coenzyme Q 10 improves mitochondrial respiration in patients with mitochondrial cytopathies. *Cell Mol Biol* 43(5):741-49.

Beharka, A. A., et al. 1997. Age related increase in macrophage (MO) nitric oxide (NO) production is decreased by vitamin E (E) supplementation. *FASEB J* 11(3)A449.

Li, D., et al. 2001. Different isoforms of tocopherols enhance nitric oxide synthase phosphorylation and inhibit human platelet aggregation and lipid peroxidation: implications in therapy with vitamin E. *J Cardiovasc Pharmacol Ther* 6:155-161.

Jiang, Q., et al. 2000. Gamma-tocopherol and its major metabolite, in contrast to alpha-tocopherol, inhibit cyclooxygenase activity in macrophages and epithelial cells. *Proc Natl Acad Science* 97(21):11494-9.

McDonald SR, S Sohal R, Forster MJ. 2005. Concurrent administration of coenzyme Q(10) and alpha-tocopherol improves learning in aged mice. *Free Radic Biol Med.* 15;38(6):729-36.

Morris, M. C., et al. Relation of the tocopherol forms to incident Alzheimer's disease and to cognitive change. *Am J Clin Nutr* 81:508-514.

Newaz, M. A., and N. N. 1999. Effect of gamma-tocotrienol on blood pressure, lipid peroxidation and total antioxidant status in spontaneously hypertensive rats (SHR). *Clin Exp Hypertens* 21(8):1297-313.

Osakada, F. 2004. Alpha-tocotrienol provides the most potent neuroprotection among vitamin E analogs on cultured striatal neurons. *Neuropharmacology* 47(6):904-15.

Qureshi, A. A. 2000. Isolation and identification of novel tocotrienols from rice bran with hypocholesterolemic, antioxidant, and antitumor properties. *J Agric Food Chem* 48(8):3130-40.

Schmidt, R. 1998. Vitamin E may help aging memory. Reuters Health *J Amer Ger Soc* 46:1407-1410.

Shults, C. W., 2003. Coenzyme Q10 in neurodegenerative diseases. *Curr Med Chem* 10(19):1917-21.

Tanyel, M. C., and L. D. Mancano. 1997. Neurologic findings in vitamin E deficiency. *Am Fam Phys* 55(1):197-201.

Theriault, A., et al. 1999. Tocotrienol: a review of its therapeutic potential. *Clin Biochem* 32(5):309-19.

Wolf, G. 1997. Gamma-tocopherol: an efficient protector of lipids against nitric oxide-initiated peroxidative damage. *Nutr Rev* 55(10):376-78.

GINKGO BILOBA

Cognitive-Enhancing Effects

Cohen-Salmon, C. et al. 1997. Effects of ginkgo biloba extract (EGb 761) on learning and possible actions on aging. *J. Physiol Paris,* 91(6):291-300.

Gessner, B., A. Voelp, and M. Klasser, M. 1985. Study of the long-term action of a ginkgo biloba extract on vigilance and mental performance as determined by means of quantitative pharmoco-EGG and psychometric measurements. *Arzneimittelforschung* 35(9):1459-65.

Kennedy, D. O., et al. 2002. Modulation of cognition and mood following administration of single doses of ginkgo biloba, ginseng, and a ginkgo/ginseng combination to healthy young adults. *Physiol Behav* 15;75(5):739-51.

Hindmarch, I. 1986. Activity of ginkgo biloba extract on short-term memory. *Presse Med* 25;15(31):1592-4.

Kanowoski, S., et al. 1996. Proof of efficacy of the ginkgo biloba special extract EGb 761 in out-patients suffering from mild to moderate primary degenerative dementia of the Alzheimer type or multi-infarct dementia. *Pharmcopsychiatry* 29(2):47-56.

Rigney, U. et al. 1999. The effects of acute doses of standardized ginkgo biloba extract on memory and psychomotor performance in volunteers. *Phytother Res* 13:408-15.

Soholm, B. 1998. Clinical improvement of memory and other cognitive functions by ginkgo biloba: review of relevant literature. *Adv Ther* 15(1)54-65.

Subhan, Z., and I. Hindmarch. 1984. The psychopharmacological effects of Ginkgo biloba extract in normal healthy volunteers. *Intrernational J of Pharmacological Research* IV, 89-93.

Warot, D., et al. 1991. Comparative effects of ginkgo biloba extracts on psychomotor performances and memory in healthy subjects. *Therapie* 46(1):33-6.

Wesnes, K. A., et al. 2000. The memory enhancing effects of a ginkgo biloba/panax ginseng combination in healthy middle-aged volunteers. *Psychopharmacology* 152(4):353-61.

Neuroprotective

Bastianetto, S. 2000. The Ginkgo biloba extract (EGb 761) protects hippocampal neurons against cell death induced by B-amyloid. *Eur J Neurosci* 12:1882-1890.

Guidetti, C., et al. 2001. Prevention of neuronal cell damage induced by oxidative stress in-vitro: effect of different Ginkgo biloba extracts. *J Pharmacology* 53(3):387-92.

Oyama, Y., et al.1996. Ginkgo biloba extract protects brain neurons against oxidative stress induced by hydrogen peroxide. *Brain Research* 712:349-352.

Rapin, J. R., I. Lamproglou, and K. Drieu. 1994. Demonstration of the anti-stress activity of an extract of ginkgo biloba. *Gen Pharmacol* 25(5):1009-16.

Rong, Y. 1996. Ginkgo biloba attenuates oxidative stress in macrophages and endothelial cells. *Free Radic Biol Med* 20(1):121-7.

Sastre, J. 1998. Ginkgo biloba prevents mitochondrial aging by protecting against oxidative stress. *Free Radical Biology & Medicine* Vol 24(2):298-304

Yao, Z., K. Drieu, and V. Papadopoulos. 2001. The ginkgo biloba extract EGb 761 rescues the PC12 neuronal cells from beta-amyloid-induced cell death by inhibiting the formation of beta-amyloid-derived diffusible neurotoxic ligands. *Brain Research* 889(1-2):181-90.

Ginseng—Panax

Benishin, C. G., 1992. Actions of ginsenoside Rb1 on choline uptake in central cholinergic nerve endings. *Neurochem Int* 21(1):1-5.

Benishin, C.G., 1990. Ginsenosides Rb1 and Rg1 increase central nervous system cholinergic metabolism. Recent Advances in Ginseng Studies. Tokyo: Hirokawa, 1990, 139-143.

Liu, M. 1996. Studies on the anti-aging and nootropic effects of ginsenoside Rg1 and its mechanisms of actions. *Sheng Li Ko Hsueh Chin Chan* 27(2):139-42.

Lyon, M. R., et al. 2001. Effects of the herbal extract combination panax quinquefolium and ginkgo biloba on attention-deficit hyperactivity disorder: a pilot study. *J Psychiatry Neuroscience* 26(3):221-8.

Petkov, V.D., and A. H. Mosharrof. 1987. Effects of standardized ginseng extract on learning, memory and physical capabilities. *Am J Chin Med.* 15(1-2):19-29.

Rudakewich, M., F. Ba, and C. G.2001. Benishin CG. Neurotrophic and neuroprotective actions of ginsenosides Rb(1) and Rg(1). *Planta Med* 67(6):533-7.

Vuksan, V. 2000. American ginseng may help control diabetes. *Archives of Internal Medicine* 160:1009-1013.

Wang, A., et al. 1995. Effects of Chinese ginseng root and stem-leaf saponins on learning; memory and biogenic monoamines of brain in rats. *Zhongguo, Zhong Yao Za Zhi* 20(8):493-5.

Green Tea (ECGC)

Hong, J. T., et al. 2000. Neuroprotective effect of green tea extract in experimental ischemia-reperfusion brain injury. *Brain Res Bull* 53(6):743-749.

Huperzine A

Cheng, D. H., and X. C. Tang. 1998. Comparative studies of huperzine A on behavior and cholinesterase activities. *Pharmacol Biochem Behav* 60(2):377-86.

Lu, W.H., J. Shou, and X. C. Tang. 1988. Improving effect of huperzine A in aged rats and adult rats with experimental cognitive impairment. *Acta Pharmacol Sin* 91:11–15.

Pilotaz, F., and P. Masson. 1999. Huperzine A: an acetylcholinesterase inhibitor with high pharmacological potential. *Ann Pharm Fr* 57(5):363-73.

Tang, X. C., et al. 1989. Effect of huperzine A: a new cholinesterase inhibitor, on the central cholinergic system of the rat. *J Neurosci Res* 24:276-285.

Ved, H. S., et al. 1997.Huperzine-A, a potential therapeutic agent for dementia, reduces neuronal cell death caused by glutamine. *Neurorepor,* 8(4):963-8.

Wang, L.M., Y. F. Han, and X. C. Tang. 2000. Huperzine A improves cognitive deficits caused by chronic cerebral hypoperfusion in rats. *Eur J Pharmacol* 398(1):65-72.

Wang, R., H. Y. Zhang, and X. C. Tang. 2001. Huperzine A attenuates cognitive dysfunction and neuronal degeneration caused by beta-amyloid protein-(1-40) in rat. *Eur J Pharmacol* 421(3):149-56.

Zhang, R. W. 1991. Positive effects of Huperzine A in the treatment of senile memory disorder. *Chung Kuo Yao Li Hsueh Pao* 12(3):250-2.

Zhu, X.D. and E. Giacobini. 1995. Second generation cholinesterase inhibitors: effect of (L)-huperzine-A on cortical biogenic amines. *J Neurosci Res* 41:828-835.

Idebenone — Aanalog of CoQ10

Gutzmann H, Kuhl KP, Hadler D, et al. 2002. Safety and efficacy of idebenone versus tacrine in patients with Alzheimer's disease: results of a randomized, double-blind, parallel-group multicenter study. *Pharmacopsychiatry* (Germany),35(1) p12

Minerals

Anderson, RA. Roussel, AM; Zouari, N; et al. 2001. Potential antioxidant effects of zinc and chromium supplementation. *J Amer Coll Nutr* 20:212-218.

Gebrewold, E. 1998. Alcohol-induced vascular damage of brain is ameliorated by administration of magnesium. *Alcohol* 15(2):95-103.

MIT Tech Talk. 2004. Magnesium may reverse middle age memory loss. http://web.mit.edu/newsoffice/2004/magnesium.html/.

Melatonin

Feng, Z., Zhang, J.T. 2004 Protective effect of melatonin on beta-amyloid-induced apoptosis in rat astroglioma c6 cells and its mechanism. *Free Radic Biol Med.* 1;37(11):1790-801.

Jean-Louis, G., von Gizycki, H, Zizi, F. 1998 Melatonin effects on sleep, mood, and cognition in elderly with mild cognitive impairment. *J Pineal Res*;25(3):177-83

Kim, Y. S. et al. 1998. Melatonin protects 6-OHDA-induced neuronal death of nigrostrial dopaminergic system. *Neuroreport* 9(10):2387-90.

Yamamoto, H.A., Mohanan, P.V. 2003. Ganglioside GT1B and melatonin inhibit brain mito-chondrial DNA damage and seizures induced by kainic acid in mice. *Brain Res.* 21;964(1):100-6.

Phan, O., D. J. Kennaway, and D. Dawson. 1998. Effect of daytime oral melatonin adminsistra-tion on neurobehavioral performance in humans. *J Pineal Res* 25(1):47.

Wang XC, Zhang J, Yu X, Han L, Zhou ZT, Zhang Y, Wang JZ. 2005. Prevention of isopro-terenol-induced tau hyperphosphorylation by melatonin in the rat. *Sheng Li Xue Bao.* 25;57(1):7-12

N-Acetyl-Cysteine

Xiong, Y., P. L. Peterson, and C. P. Lee. 1999. Effect of N-acetylcysteine on mitochondrial func-tion following traumatic brain injury in rats. *J Neurotrauma* 16(11):1067-82.

Kheir-Eldin, A. A. 2001. Protective effect of vitamin E, beta-carotene and N-acetylcysteine from the brain oxidative stress induced in rats by lipopolysaccharide. *Int J Biochem Cell Biol* 33(5):475-82.

Phosphatidyl Serine

Borghese, C. M., et al. 1993. Phosphatidyl serine increases hippocampal synaptic efficacy. *Brain Research* 31:697-700.

Cenacchi, T., et al. 1993. Cognitive decline in the elderly: a double-blind, placebo-controlled multicenter study on efficacy of phosphatidylserine administration. *Aging* 5(2):123-33.

Crook, T. H., et al. 1991. Effects of phosphatidylserine in age-associated memory impairment. *Neurology* 41:644-649.

Resveratrol

Zhuang, H., et al. 2003. Potential mechanism by which resveratrol, a red wine constituent, pro-tects neurons. *Ann N Y Acad Sci* 993: 276-88.

Vigili, M., and A. Contestabile. 2000. Partial neuroprotection of in vivo excitotoxic brain dam-age by chronic administration of the red wine antioxidant agent, trans-resveratrol in rats. *Neurosci Lett* (2-3):123-26.

Wang, Y. J., F. He., and X. L. Li. 2003. The neuroprotection of resveratrol in the experimental cerebral ischemia. *Zhonghua Yi Xue Za Zhi* 83(7):534-6.

Tyrosine

Hale, B., M. J. Stillman, and H. R. Lieberman. 1996. Tyrosine administration prevents hypoxia-induced decrements in learning and memory. *Physiol Behav* 59(4-5):867-71.

Moosman, B. 2000. Cytoprotective antioxidant function of tyrosine and tryptophan residues in transmembrane proteins. *Eur J Biochem* 267(18):5687-92.

Shurtleff, D., et al. 1994. Tyrosine reverses a cold-induced working memory deficit in humans, helps mental performance under stress. *Pharmacol Biochem Beha* 47(4):935-41.

Vinpocetine

Hindmarch, I. 1985. Psychopharmacological effects of vinpocetine in normal healthy volunteers. *Eur J Clin Pharmacol* 28(5):567-71.

Pereira, C. A., et al. 2003. Neuroprotection strategies: effect of vinpocetine in vitro oxidative stress models. *Acta Med Port* 16(6):401-406.

Pereira, C., P. Agostinho, and C. R. Oliveira. 2000. Vinpocetine attenuates the metabolic dysfunction induced by amyloid beta-peptides in PC12 cells. *Free Radic Res* 33(5):497-506.

Polich, J., and R. Gloria. 2001. Cognitive effects of a ginkgo biloba/vinpocetine compound in normal adults: systematic assessment of perception, attention and memory. *Hum Psychopharmacol* 16(5):409-416.

Santos, M. S., et al. 2000. Synaptosomal response to oxidative stress: effect of vinpocetine. *Free Radic Res* 32(1):57-66.

NEUROHORMONES AND NEUROTRANSMITTERS

Birge, S. J., et al. 1994. The role of estrogen deficiency in the aging central nervous system. *Treatment of the Postmenopausal Woman: Basic and Clinical Aspects.* New York: Raven Pressm 1994.

Blasberg, M. E., et al. 1996. Dynamics of working memory across the estrous cycle. *Abstr Soc Neurosci* 22:547:1386.

Flood, J. F., et al. 1995. Age-related decrease of plasma testosterone: replacement improves age-related impairment of learning and memory. *Physiol Behav* 57(4):669-73.

Flynn, M. A., et al. 1999. Dehydroepiandrosterone replacement in aging humans. *J. Clin Endocrinol Metab* 84(5):527-1533.

Gouras, G. K., et al. 2000. Testosterone reduces neuronal secretion of Alzheimer's beta-amyloid peptides. *Proc Natl Acad Sci USA* 97(3):1202-5.

Halbreich, U., et al. 1995. Possible acceleration of age effects on cognition following menopause. *J.Psychiatr Res* 29(3):153-63.

Morales, A. J., et al. 1998. The effects of six months treatment with a 100 mg daily dose of dehydroepiandrosterone (DHEA) on circulating sex steroids, body composition and muscle strength in age-advanced men and women. *Clin Endocrinol* 49(4):421-432.

Stolk, R. P., et al. 1997. Insulin and cognitive function in an elderly population. The Rotterdam Study. *Diabetes Care* 20(5):792-5.

Tanapat, P., et al. 1999. Estrogen stimulates a transient increase in the number of neurons in the dentate gyrus of the adult female rat. *J Neurosci* 5792-5801.

Neurotransmitters and Nerve Growth Factors (NGFs)

Amenta, F., et al. 1993. Cholinergic neurotransmission in the hippocampus of aged rats. *Academy Science* 695:311-3.

Cheng, D., and X. C. Tang. 1997. Orally active NGF (nerve growth factor) synthesis stimulator: potential therapeutic agents in Alzheimer's disease. *Behav Brain Res* 83(1-2):117-22.

Harrison, A. A., et al. 1997. Central 5-HT depletion enhances impulsive responding without affecting the accuracy of attentional performance: interactions with dopaminergic mechanisms. *Psychopharmacology* 133(4):329-42.

Volkow., N. D. et al. 1998. Association between decline in brain dopamine activity with age and cognitive and motor impairment in healthy individuals. *Am J Psychiatry* 155(3):344-9.

PHYSICAL EXERCISE, BRAIN HEALTH, AND COGNITIVE PERFORMANCE

Emery, C. F., F. A. Huppert, and R. L. Schein. 1995. Relationships among age, exercise, health, and cognitive function in a British sample. *Gerontologist* 35(3):378-85.

Isaacs, K. R., et al. 1992. Exercise and the brain: angiogenesis in the adult rat cerebellum after vigorous physical activity and motor skill learning. *J Cereb Blood Flow Metan* 12(1):110-9.

Kramer, A., 1999. Walking improves mental processing. *Nature* 400:418-419.

Kramer, A. 1999. Improvement in aerobic fitness selectively boosts neurocognitive function. *Nature* 400:418-419.

Laurin, D., et al. 2001. Physical activity and risk of cognitive impairment and dementia in elderly persons. *Arch Neurol* 58(3):498-504.

Lupinacci, N. S., 1993. Age and physical activity effects on reaction time and digit symbol substitution performance in cognitively active adults. *Res Q Exerc Sport* 64(2):144-50.

Van Praag, H., G. Kempermann, G., and F. H. Gage. 1999. Running increases cell proliferation and neurogenesis in the adult mouse dentate gyrus. *Nat Neurosci* 2(3):266-70.

MENTAL EXERCISE AND BRAIN STIMULATION, EDUCATION, ENVIRONMENTAL ENRICHMENT, NOVELTY AND NEUROGENESIS

Bennett, D. A., et al. 2003. Education modifies the relation of AD pathology to level of cognitive function in older persons. *Neurology* 60:1909-1915.

During, M. 1999. A stimulating environment protects brain cells against death. *Nature Medicine* 5:448-453.

Huggins, C. 1999. Creative play builds coping skills, lowers stress. *Creativity Research J* 12:129-139.

Leake, J; 2001. Cyber-games make children brighter. *Sunday Times* Jul 22, 2001.

Mattson, M. P., 2000. Neuroprotective signaling and the aging brain: take away my food and let me run. *J Brain Res* 886(1-2):47-53.

Pham, T. M., et al.1997. Effects of neonatal stimulation on later cognitive function and hippocampal nerve growth factor. *Behav Brain Res* 86(1):113-20.

Riley, K. P., et al. 2005. Early life linguistic ability, late life cognitive function, and neuropathology: findings from the Nun Study. *Neurobiol Aging* 26(3):341-7.

Van Praag, H., G. Kempermann, and F. H. Gage. 2000. Neural consequences of environmental enrichment. *Nat Rev Neurosci* 1(3):191-8.

Viola, H., et al. 2000. Phosphorylated cAMP response element-binding protein as a molecular marker of memory processing in rat hippocampus: effect of novelty. *J Neurosci* 20(23):112.

Wilson, R., et al. 2002. Participation in cognitively stimulating activities and risk of incident Alzheimer Disease. *JAMA* 287:742-748.

Young, D., et al. 1999. Environmental enrichment inhibits spontaneous apoptosis, prevents seizures and is neuroprotective. *NatureMedicine* 5(4):448-53

Neurogenesis

Chen, G., et al. 2000. Enhancement of hippocampal neurogenesis by lithium. *J Neurochem* 75(4):1729-34.

Duman, R. S., S. Nakagawa, and J. Malberg. 2001. Regulation of adult neurogenesis by antidepressant treatment. *Neuropsychopharmacology* 26(6):836-44.

Gage, F. 2002. Neurogenesis in the adult brain. *J Neurosci* 22(3);612-613.

Gould, G,, et al. 1999. Neurogenesis in adulthood: a possible role in learning. *Trends in Cognitive Sciences* 3:5:186-192.

Kempermann, G. 2002. Why new neurons? Possible functions for adult hippocampal neurogenesis. *J Neurosci* 22(3):635-638.

Kempermann, G., H. G. Kuhn, and F. H. Gage. 2001. Activity-dependent regulation of neuronal plasticity and self repair. *Prog Brain Res* 127;35-48.

Kempermann, G., H. G. Kuhn, and F. H. Gage. 1997. More hippocampal neurons (neurogenesis) living in an enriched environment. *Nature* 386:493-495.

Lee, J. et al. 2000. Dietary restriction increases the number of newly generated neural cells, and induces BDNF expression in the dentate gyrus of rats. *Eur J Neuroscience* 15(2):99-198.

Lemaire, V. 1999. Behavioural trait of reactivity to novelty is related to hippocampal neurogenesis. *Eur J Neuroscience* 11(11):4006-14.

Takahasho, J., T. D. Palmer, and F. H. Gage. 1999. Retinoic acid and neurotrophins collaborate to regulate neurogenesis in adult-derived neural stem cell cultures. *J Neurobiol* 38(1):65-81.

Tanapat, P., et al. 1999. Estrogen stimulates a transient increase in the number of neurons in the dentate gyrus of the adult female rat. *J Neurosci* 19:5792-5801.

Van Praag, H., et al. 1999. Running enhances neurogenesis, learning, and long-term potentiation in mice. *Proc Natl Acad Sciences* 99(23):13427-31.

BRAIN SPEED, SPEED OF PROCESSING AND REACTION TIME

Speed and IQ, Cognition, Memory, Health, and Longevity

Carolien, H. 1999. Cognitive functioning and health as determinants of morality in an older population *Amer J of Epidemiology* 150(9):p978-86

Deary, I. J., and G. Der. 2005. Reaction time explains IQ's association with death. *Psychological Science*: p64-69.

Earles, J. L. and A. W. Kertsten. 1999. Processing speed and adult age differences in activity memory. *Exp Aging Res* 25(3):243-53.

Edwards. J. D., et al. 2002. Transfer of a speed of processing intervention to near and far cognitive functions. *Gerontology* 48(5):329-40.

Fozard, J.L., 1994. Age differences and changes in reaction time: the Baltimore Longitudinal Study of Aging. *J Gerontol* 49(4):179-89.

Fry, A. F., and S. Hale. 2000. Relationships among processing speed, working memory, and fluid intelligence in children. *Biol Psychol* 54(1-3):1-34.

Houx, P. J., and J. Jolles. 1993. Age-related decline of psychomotor speed; effects of age, brain health, sex, and education. *Percept Motor Skills* 76(1):195-211.

Jackson, M. D. 1979. Brain speed of processing correlates with reading speed. *J Exp Psychol* 108(2):151-81.

Jensen, A. 1997. Reaction time correlates of intelligence. *Intelligence* 3:121-126.

Kirby, N. H., and T. Nettelbeck, T. 1989. Reaction time and inspection time as measures of intellectual ability. *Pergamon Press* 10(1)11-14.

Klimesch, W., et al. 1996. Alpha frequency, reaction time, and the speed of processing information. *J Clinical Neurophysiol* 13(6):511-8.

Kranzler, J. 1994. Speed and efficiency of elemental information processing in highly complex cognitive tasks better in high IQ gifted individuals. *Contemporary Educational Psychology* 19:447-459.

Kyllonen, P., and R. Christal. 1990. Reasoning ability based on working-memory capacity and speed. Air Force Learning Abilities Measurement Program. *Intelligence* 14:389-433.

Lupinacci, N. S., et al. 1993. Age and physical activity effects on reaction time and digit symbol substitution performance in cognitively active adults. *Res Q Exerc Sport* 64(2):144-50.

Morganthaler, J. 1998. The missing method – Thinkfast and speed-of-processing tests help tailor brain nutrient program for optimal mental performance. *Smart Life News* 6(4)34.

Nettelbeck, T., and N. H. Kirby. 1983. Timed performance (speed of processing) correlations with Intelligence. *Intelligence* 7: 39-52.

Pavlik, V. N., et al. 2003. Relation between cognitive function and mortality in middle-aged adults: the atherosclerosis risk in communities study. *Am J Epidemiol* 157(4):327-34.

Rijsdijk, F. V., P. A. Vernon, and D. I. Boomsma. 1988. The genetic basis of the relation between speed-of-information-processing and IQ. *Behav Brain Res* 95(1):77-84.

Sherwood, D. E., and D. J. Selder. 1979. Cardiorespiratory health, reaction time and aging. *Med Sci Sports* 11(2):186-9.

Smits, C. H., et al. 1999. Cognitive functioning and health as determinants of morality in an older population. *Am J Epidemiol* 150(9):978-86.

Weissberg, R., H. A. Ruff, and K. R. Lawson. 1990. The usefulness of reaction time tasks in studying attention and organization of behavior in young children. *J Dev Behav Pediatr* 11(2):59-64.

Ylikoski, R., et al. 1993. White matter changes in healthy elderly persons correlate with attention and speed of mental processing. *Arch Neurol;* 50:818-824.

ALPHA BRAIN BREAK—CAT NAPS, MEDITATION, YOGA — AND COGNITIVE HEALTH AND PERFORMANCE

Edwards, L. 2003. Meditation as medicine. Benefits go beyond relaxation. *Adv Nurse Pract* 11(5):49-52.

Cranson, R. W.; Orme-Johnson, D. W.; Gackenbach, J.; Dillbeck, M.C.; Jones, C. H.; and ALEXANDER, C. N. 1991. Transcendental Meditation and improved performance on intelligence-related measures: A longitudinal study. *Personality and Individual Differences* 12(10): 1105-1116,

Goddard, P. H. 1992. Transcendental Meditation as an intervention in the aging of Neurocognitive Function: Reduced Age-Related Declines of P300 Latencies in elderly practitioners. Summary of Doctoral Dissertation, Maharishi International University, U.S.A. *Dissertation Abstracts International*, 53 (6):3189B

Kamei, T. 2000. Decrease in serum cortisol during yoga exercise is correlated with alpha brain wave activation. *Percept Mot Skills* 90(3-1):1027-32.

Maclean, C. R. K.; Walton, K. G.; Wenneberg, S. R.; Levitsky, D.K.; Mandarino, J. V.; Waziiri, R.; and Scheneider, R. H. 1994. Altered responses of cortisol, GH, TSH, and testosterone to acute stress after four months' practice of Transcendental Meditation (TM). Presented at the New York Academy of Sciences meeting on Brain Corticosteroid Receptors: Studies on the Mechanism, Function, and Neurotoxicity of Corticosteroid Action, Arlington, VA, March2-5,

Schwartz, E. 1979 The effects of the Transcendental Meditation programon strength of the nervous system, perceptual reactance, reaction time, and auditory threshold. Master's thesis (abbr.), Department of Exercise Science, University of Massachusetts, Amherst, Massachusetts, U.S.A.

Sudsuang, R., V. Chentanez, and K. Veluvan. 1991. Effects of Buddhist meditation on serum cortisol and total protein levels, blood pressure, pulse rate, lung volume and reaction time. *Physiol Behav* 50(3):543-8.

Tacon, A. M., et al. 2003. Mindfulness meditation, anxiety reduction, and heart disease: a pilot study. *Fam Community Health* 26(1):25-33.

LIFESTYLE FACTORS—POSITIVE AND NEGATIVE EFFECTS OF ALCOHOL, DRUGS AND MEDICATIONS, AND SLEEP

Positive Effects of Moderate Alcohol Use

Galanis, D. 2000. A drink a day may keep mental decline away. *Amer J of Public Health* 90:1254-1259.

Halpern, M. J., et al. 1998. Red-wine polyphenols and inhibition of platelet aggregation: possible mechanisms, and potential use in health promotion and disease prevention. *J Int Med Res* 26:171-80.

Renaud, S., and M. de Lorgeril. 1992. Wine, alcohol, platelets, and the French paradox for coronary heart disease. *Lancet* 339,1523-26.

Vigili, M., and A. Contestabile, A. 2000. Partial neuroprotection of in vivo excitotoxic brain damage by chronic administration of the red wine antioxidant agent, trans-resveratrol in rats. *Neurosci Lett* 281(2-3):123-26.

Zuccala, G., et al. 2001. Dose-related impact of alcohol consumption on cognitive function in advanced age: results of a multicenter survey. *Alcohol Clin Exp Res* 25(12):1743-8.

Negative Impact of Alcohol and Other Recreational Drugs

Gebrewold, E. et al. 1998. Alcohol-induced vascular damage of brain is ameliorated by administration of magnesium. *Alcohol* 15(2):95-103.

Lieber, C. S. 2000. Alcohol: its metabolism and interaction with nutrients. *Ann Rev Nutrition* 20:395-430.

Mansouri, A. 2001. Acute ethanol administration oxidatively damages and depletes mitochondrial DNA in mouse liver, brain, heart, and skeletal muscles: protective effects of antioxidants. *J Pharmacol Exp Ther* 298(2):737-43.

Sun, A. Y., and G. Y. Sun. 2001. Ethanol and oxidative mechanisms in the brain. *J Biomed Sci* 8(1):37-43.

Parrott, A. C., et al. 1998. Cognitive performance in recreational users of MDMA or 'ecstasy': evidence for memory deficits. *J Psychopharmacology* 12(1):79-83.

Caffeine

Deslandes AC, Veiga H, Cagy M, et al. 2004.Effects of caffeine on visual evoked potential (P300) and neuromotor performance. *Arq Neuropsiquiatr* (Brazil) 62(2B) p385-90

Jarvis, M. J. 1993. Does caffeine intake enhance absolute levels of cognitive performance? *Psychopharmacology* 110(1-2):45-52.

Korkotian, E. 1999. Release of calcium from stores alters the morphology of dendritic spines in cultured hippocampal neurons. *Proc Natl Acad of Sci* 96(21) 12068-72.

Kaasinen V, Aalto S, Nagren K, et al. 2004. Dopaminergic effects of caffeine in the human striatum and thalamus. *Neuroreport* (England) 15(2) p281-5

Smith A, Brice C, Nash J, et al. 2003. Caffeine and central noradrenaline: effects on mood, cognitive performance, eye movements and cardiovascular function. *J Psychopharmacol* (United States)17(3) p283-92

Sleep

Maquet, P. 2000. To sleep perchance to...lay down memories. *Nature Neuroscience* 3:831-836.

Stickgold, R. 2000. Sleepy brains have trouble forming memories. *Nature Neuroscience* 3:1237-1238, 1335-1339.

Weinger, M., and S. Ancoli-Israel. 2002. Sleep deprivation and clinical performance. *JAMA* 287(8):955.

Williamson, A. M., and A. M. Feyer. 2000. Moderate sleep deprivation produces impairments in cognitive and motor performance equivalent to legally prescribed levels of alcohol intoxication. *Occup Environ Med* 57(10):649-55.

Zwillich, T. 2000. Early to rise raises GPA. *J of Amer College Health* 49:125-130.

Statins May Increase Risk of Memory Loss, Yet Protect Against Alzheimer's

Abad-Rodriguez, J. et al. 2004. Neuronal membrane cholesterol loss enhances amyloid peptide generation. *J. Cell Biol* 167:953-960.

Black, S. L. 2005. Serum cholesterol and visuomotor speed: inverse or direct association? *Am J Clin Nutr* 81: 537-538.

Cole SL, Grudzien A, Manhart IO, Kelly BL, Oakley H, Vassar R. Statins cause intracellular accumulation of amyloid precursor protein, beta-secretase-cleaved fragments, and amyloid beta-peptide via an isoprenoid-dependent mechanism. *J Biol Chem.* 2005 May 13;280(19):18755-70

Graveline, D. 2004. Lipitor® Thief of Memory. Statin Drugs and the Misguided War on Cholesterol. Haverford, PA: Infinity, 2004.

Mortensen, S.A. 1997. Statins (HMG-CoA reductase inhibitors) decrease serum coenzyme (Co) Q10 levels. *Mol Aspects Med* 18:137-44.

Muldoon, M. F., et al. 2000. Effects of lovastatin on cognitive function and psychological well-being. *Amer J of Medicine* 108:538-546.

Wolozin, B. et al, 2007, "Simvastatin is associated with a reduced incidence of dementia". *BioMed Central (BMC) Medicine*, July, 5:20, http://www.biomedcentral.com/1741-7015/5/20

Wolozin, B. et al , 2000 Decreased Prevalence of Alzheimer Disease Associated With 3-Hydroxy-3-Methyglutaryl Coenzyme A Reductase Inhibitors. *Arch Neurol.* 57:1439-1443.